THE PARENT'S HANDBOOK TO UNSCHOOLING YOURSELF

of related interest

A Different Way to Learn
Neurodiversity and Self-Directed Education
Naomi Fisher
ISBN 978 1 83997 363 5
eISBN 978 1 83997 364 2
audiobook ISBN 978 1 39982 376 0

Parenting Rewired
How to Raise a Happy Autistic Child in a Very Neurotypical World
Danielle Punter and Charlotte Chaney
ISBN 978 1 83997 072 6
eISBN 978 1 83997 073 3
audiobook ISBN 978 1 39981 202 3

A Different Kind of Parenting
Neurodivergent Families Finding a Way Through Telling Together
Eliza Fricker
ISBN 978 1 80501 295 5
eISBN 978 1 80501 296 2

Where Do I Start?
How to Navigate the Emotional Journey of Autism Parenting
Kate Laine-Toner
ISBN 978 1 83997 552 3
eISBN 978 1 83997 553 0

The Parent's Handbook to
Unschooling Yourself

A Mindful Guide to Embracing a New Way of Living and Learning With Your Child

Esther Jones

Jessica Kingsley Publishers
London and Philadelphia

First published in Great Britain in 2025 by Jessica Kingsley Publishers
An imprint of John Murray Press

1

Copyright © Esther Jones 2025

The right of Esther Jones to be identified as the Author of the Work has been asserted by her in accordance with the Copyright, Designs and Patents Act 1988.

Front cover image source: Shutterstock®. The cover image is for illustrative purposes only, and any person featuring is a model.

All rights reserved. No part of this publication may be reproduced, stored in a retrieval system, or transmitted, in any form or by any means without the prior written permission of the publisher, nor be otherwise circulated in any form of binding or cover other than that in which it is published and without a similar condition being imposed on the subsequent purchaser.

A CIP catalogue record for this title is available from the
British Library and the Library of Congress

ISBN 978 1 80501 275 7
eISBN 978 1 80501 276 4

Printed and bound in Great Britain by Clays Ltd

Jessica Kingsley Publishers' policy is to use papers that are natural, renewable and recyclable products and made from wood grown in sustainable forests. The logging and manufacturing processes are expected to conform to the environmental regulations of the country of origin.

Jessica Kingsley Publishers
Carmelite House
50 Victoria Embankment
London EC4Y 0DZ

www.jkp.com

John Murray Press
Part of Hodder & Stoughton Ltd
An Hachette Company

The authorised representative in the EEA is Hachette Ireland,
8 Castlecourt Centre, Dublin 15, D15 XTP3, Ireland (email: info@hbgi.ie)

Contents

Preface 9

Introduction 13
    Introducing the parents   16
    How to use this book   23

Part 1: Learning about learning   25

1. How do children learn? 27
    Born to learn   30
    The power of intrinsic motivation   32
    Our own internal reward system   33
    A learning frame of mind   34
    Learning and playfulness   36

2. Learning to be themselves. 43
    Living life in all its fullness   44
    Our child's internal navigation system   44
    How our childhood experiences affect us   45
    Self-Determination Theory: driven by our need to grow and be fulfilled   46
    Autonomy   46
    Competence   54
    Connection   56

3. **What does self-directed learning look like in action?** 61
   It's about the process, not the outcome   62
   How will you know your child is learning?   73
   If you don't pay attention, you might miss it   76

4. **Holding the space for your child** 81
   Accompanying our children on a journey   82
   It's hard to let go of what we think it should all look like 84
   What qualities do we bring to the space?   86
   It may feel neglectful at first   92
   Being with your child all day   94

5. **But what do I actually do?** 99
   There are no fixed rules   99
   Facilitate their interests   100
   Bring the world in   102
   Learn alongside them   104
   Prioritize conversation   104
   Strew about potential things of interest   105
   Help shift the gears   106
   Help to create structure   106
   Help them regulate and reconnect   110
   Facilitate friendships and community   110
   Help them navigate the wider world   112

6. **Navigating technology** 115
   Without school in the picture, the dynamics shift   116
   What is screen time anyway?   117
   The richness of technology   117
   Online and offline, it's all real life   123
   Keeping our children safe and healthy – playing the long game 123

7. **How fear keeps us going in circles** 135
   What is fear?   136
   Other people's scrutiny   143
   Sitting in uncharted waters   144
   How does fear hold us back?   145
   Welcome discomfort!   148

Part 2: The four steps to freedom — 151

8. Step 1: Pause! 153
    What triggers us — 154
    When our reactions come from a place of fear — 156
    Catastrophic thoughts — 159
    'Doing' mode and 'Being' mode — 162
    Mindfulness practices to help you find the pause button — 164
    Ways to cultivate Being mode with your child — 166

9. Step 2: Be kind 169
    Self-compassion — 170
    Why are we so hard on ourselves? — 173
    Why learning beyond school can make us hard on ourselves — 174
    We must first be good parents to ourselves — 176
    What happens when we are kind to ourselves — 177
    Self-compassion practices — 179
    Self-compassion can be surprisingly challenging — 180

10. Step 3: Be curious 185
    Discovering your child — 186
    Turn to your child for the answers — 188
    Staying present and connected — 195

11. Step 4: Engage 201
    A new space — 202
    As we shift, our children shift too — 205
    The communication dance — 206
    Engaging with needs, not solutions — 210

Part 3: Nurturing yourself through change — 217

12. Relearning to be yourself 219
    Unravelling or peeling back the layers — 219
    Take your time — 220
    Why do our children lead us there? — 220
    Giving yourself permission — 223
    Working with our practical limitations — 229

13. Practices to support you in your deschooling journey . . . 235
    Why do we need specific practices?   236
    Finding flow   243
    Other practices we can bring to our lives   246

14. Creating your community 253
    We're hard-wired for community   254
    Building a community for you and your children   256

    References 267
    Bibliography 269

Preface

When my eldest son was just a toddler, I came across a book called *How Children Learn at Home* by Alan Thomas and Harriet Pattison. It was the first time I'd ever read about children learning outside school, and I was fascinated. Two things in particular stood out for me. The first was about reading. Many parents in Thomas and Pattison's book described how their children resisted all attempts at being taught to read. Instead, they took it at their own pace, engaging with reading in the way that worked for them and, in their own time and with minimum adult intervention, became fluent readers. The age they started reading had no bearing on how well they read later or on how much they enjoyed reading. The other thing that stayed with me was a discussion between a mother, father and daughter about how one of the main sources of learning in their family was the interesting conversations that came up on car journeys. Their book is filled with hundreds of similar examples of natural, stress-free learning, but these two struck a deep chord with me.

At that time we lived in Spain, where home education inhabits a murky legal space and is considered eccentric to say the least. There didn't appear to be any viable path other than school, and anyway, despite this wonderful book, I still had some strong misgivings about what I had only ever known as 'home schooling'. However, Thomas and Pattison's book convinced me that our children had an innate drive to learn, and that we needed to keep that drive alive and well. So, for their first few years, our two sons went to a gentle, child-centred, pre-school in the mornings. Then, when my eldest son turned six, we moved a little up the coast from Barcelona, where we lived, so they could attend a new, alternative primary school. There were no obligatory lessons at this school, which was set in a lush garden with huge pine trees. They stayed there for a few years, and although we all took many wonderful things from this school, finally, and for various reasons, it felt like we'd come to the end of our time there. So we took them out and began our search for somewhere else for them and their younger sister. I wanted a place where they would feel free to be themselves and learn in their own way, while also feeling safe and held. I researched a dozen different options, we visited a couple of places, and we even contemplated moving to another city. Meanwhile, people were shocked that our children weren't at school.

For that first year, while we searched for the perfect school, my partner and I tag-teamed between work and the children, trying to figure out what this could all look like. The pressure and responsibility felt intense and, even though our children had never been to a formal school, I was frequently stressed and anxious about their learning, their friendships and the future. There were lots of ups and downs, but they got on with the things they enjoyed and showed me that they were hugely motivated to learn. Just as the parents in Thomas and Pattison's book described, at the ages of eight and nine, our sons had both gone from seeming to be non-readers to reading fluently in the space of weeks, and with almost no input from anyone else (a few years later, my daughter did the same, at the age of six). Even so, I was still jittery. My intuition and what I was seeing were telling me one thing, but it appeared to go against everything everyone else believed.

About a year into this new life, I left the business I had founded and run for more than 20 years. I was burnt out and lost, aware that for some time now I had been following someone else's notion of what success looked like. I realized that, while wanting my children to feel free to be themselves and follow their passions, I myself was following a series of 'shoulds' that felt far from authentic. While pounding the mainstream treadmill and attempting to be successful, I was painfully aware that happiness and fulfilment lay elsewhere. For some years I had also been studying mindfulness and had become a doula and Hypnobirthing practitioner, but I was so bound up in relentless expectations and busyness, that these interests only hovered on the fringes of my life.

However, through my studies and work with pregnant women and their partners, I had become fascinated by how we accompany each other through the natural processes of life. I had seen and experienced firsthand the importance of holding a woman in labour in a space that is safe, loving and trusting. And I had begun to work more closely with birth companions to help them create an environment within which their partner could feel safe and confident – not taking over and not standing back, but consciously holding space for her. I started to understand that, similarly, children need to be held in a space within which they can relax and connect with their innate confidence and drive to learn. And I realized that our role was not to direct or control what or how they learned, but to accompany them in a way that the natural process of learning could unfold.

In an attempt to find some more freedom and clarity, we moved from our little house in the town up to an old house in the hills nearby. Hugged by woodlands and looking out to the Mediterranean Sea, the house bordered on a natural park, which extended up into the hills behind. I taught Hypnobirthing and took on editing work from home while my partner often travelled for his work. We stopped looking for the perfect school and started to relax into this space. We lived in this place for almost two years and, without the outside world dictating our days, I allowed the slow process of my own healing to gather speed. Observing my children was everything I needed to understand how deeply conditioned I was in so many ways. Meditation, long morning walks into the hills above and journalling were my tools for unravelling over 20 years of striving. And as I healed and let go, I was able to see my children more clearly. Not for who they were supposed to be or who I needed them to be, but for who they were.

I saw that learning is indeed inevitable and often invisible. I was amazed every day by the depth of their knowledge and the sophistication of the themes they wanted to talk about. They became relentless researchers and challengers of conventional wisdom. New interests were born, some of which are still alive and well all these years later, and others that came and went from one week to the next. There were endless conversations and plenty of TV and gaming, much of which then led to new passions and interests. It looked nothing like I had ever imagined learning to look like. But the more I paid attention, the more I understood the validity of what they were doing and what they were getting out of things that had initially baffled me. The idea that I would ever lead the way for them now seemed absurd. The only question ever was whether we could hold them in the way they needed, or if we would try to wrest control from them in the name of good parenting. I started my blog 'A Place on a Hill' as a way to digest and document what I was seeing and learning.[1]

I also recognized in our house on the hill that we all need community, each in our own way, and that community isn't always easy to build. We had dear friends locally and in Barcelona, but in a place where all other children were at school during the day, we would probably all agree that sometimes it was too quiet. Eventually, after two years, family and community won the day and we moved back to the UK, where we now live. Here, I became a mindfulness teacher and, in 2021, I began my podcast, 'The Unschool Space'.[2] In the podcast, I chat with other parents who have taken an alternative path with their children. I have been amazed at how, no matter where in the world my guests live, so much of this experience is universal. The same themes come up over and over, and in particular, the parent's own deschooling journey. Once we start to pay attention to our children and observe how they learn, we inevitably realize that the ones who really need to learn are us.

---

1 https://aplaceonahill.com
2 https://theunschoolspace.buzzsprout.com

Introduction

You might have never planned to send your child to school, or it may still be a bit of a shock to find yourself here. Most of the parents I've talked with over the years didn't consider home education until they realized that school was not going to work for their child. In some cases that meant a young child becoming withdrawn and anxious or having explosive meltdowns in the evenings. In others, years of school refusal and increasing mental distress meant that parents simply ran out of choices. Whatever the reason for taking an alternative route, every parent I've met has done so out of a deep desire for their child to feel happy and whole.

Unschooling is based on the knowledge that children are naturally curious and capable of deep learning when emotionally engaged and given the space and autonomy to follow their own path. For a self-directed child, intrinsically motivated by what interests them, learning is joyful and fulfilling. It is not a means to somewhere else but rather an open-ended, lifelong exploration. And although learning is a large part of unschooling, it is also just the logical outcome when a child is able to live in a way that feels satisfying and authentic to them.

This is about accompanying our children in the belief that they are whole just as they are. That each of us (including ourselves) has a unique way of being in this world, and the more connected we are to our own desires and values, the happier and more satisfying our lives can be. With our support, our children can achieve a deep understanding of themselves and how they best thrive in life. They can become experts at making aligned choices, and in knowing and advocating for their own values and boundaries. This ability to live in accordance with their own inner motor and values will be with them throughout their lives, helping them live in a way that feels coherent to them.

Every now and again I come across a piece of online wisdom that says a child will need one month of deconditioning (often referred to as 'deschooling') for every year they have spent at school. I suspect it can take anything from days to months for a child to relax, find their own rhythm and connect with what they love. But children are rarely the stumbling block to learning out of school; the challenges that arise are far more likely to be all about the parents. Most of us only know about education in terms of formal school and have never seen a child learn independently, without a timetable, a curriculum or an adult in charge. We have no idea what this might look like. So, no matter how good our intentions, we tend to come unstuck, not because our child is doing anything wrong, but because our own deep conditioning around learning, parenting, and even around ourselves makes it hard for us to trust our children and the process. We get stressed and anxious that things aren't as they should be, and then we give ourselves a hard time because we don't seem to be getting it right. We can easily start a vicious circle, whereby our concerns create tension, no one really thrives, and that, in turn, feeds our concerns.

Deschooling ourselves is all about us getting beyond this deep conditioning that can so easily undermine our children and our relationship with them. It's about learning to trust ourselves and to trust our children. It can take months or even years to really get comfortable, and the gentle peeling back of layers probably lasts a lifetime. In the beginning, it can feel like a crazy roller coaster ride, with exhilarating highs and lows and mind-blowing realizations. As time moves on, it becomes a practice – a gentle and continual growing and bumping into new edges.

For most parents, deschooling is both immensely rewarding and incredibly challenging. It involves not only appreciating learning from an entirely new perspective, but changing the way we view children and parenting. It's easy for this to seem like the best decision in the world after a harmonious morning of baking and nature walks or a long political discussion around the kitchen table with your bright pre-teens. And you can sit back satisfied that it's all flowing rather nicely when you see your children happily playing with their friends or with their noses in a good book. This is exactly how you hoped it would look! But how about a morning on the PlayStation? How about when your child doesn't seem to want to do anything at all? What if Minecraft is the preferred learning tool? Or when the whole day seems to have been one long and exhausting sibling argument?

It can be hard, but the real deschooling lies in these triggering moments. That's when we make a choice. We can react with worry, anger or guilt because it wasn't supposed to be this way. Or we can take a deep breath, be kind to ourselves, let go of our preconceived notions of how we think learning and life are supposed to look, and take a closer look at what's going on. I have often thought of deschooling as mindfulness in action. It requires us to continually stop, come back to the present moment, challenge the idea that our perception is the truth, and observe how our automatic reactions impact ourselves and our children. It's hard work but this is where the magic lies. As you undo your old stories and beliefs that hold you and your child in outdated and limiting patterns, you'll see how things have room to shift and move in new and unexpected ways. As you start to hold space for your child so that they are free to fully engage in their own unique learning journey, you'll see that the learning that naturally arises is far more expansive and meaningful.

And, of course, we are whole people too. As you learn to trust your child, you will undoubtedly find yourself looking at many aspects of your own life through that same lens. You'll become more aware of when you are acting in ways that are aligned with your own happiness and when you're not, and you'll learn what you need to include in your days so that you too feel resourced and fulfilled. In order to accompany our children in a way that is authentic and healthy, we have no choice but to also tend to ourselves.

This book doesn't offer a blueprint for learning beyond school, because every family is unique, and your journey won't look like anyone else's. Just as we adults are a vast array of different people, so are our children. Although that might feel a little nerve-wracking, it also means that you have the freedom to create a life within which your whole family can thrive. So, rather than a book of answers, this is really a book of questions and practices, which, I hope, will help guide you to finding your own answers. Use it in whatever way feels most helpful to you, but I would recommend incorporating the practices as you go, and spending some time with the journal prompts at the end of each chapter to help you dig as deep as you want or need to go.

For the sake of clarity, the parenting and learning approach I talk about in this book would commonly be described as 'unschooling'. The term was coined in the 1970s by John Holt, an American educator and author who was a key figure in the education reform movement and advocated for alternatives to traditional schooling. He believed in child-led, interest-based learning, and wrote several books, including *How Children Learn*. In my work, I mostly use the term 'unschooling', and sometimes 'self-directed learning' or just 'learning beyond school', and I use those terms interchangeably. In the UK, the term 'home education' is often used as an umbrella for many different styles and outlooks. It doesn't really matter what labels we use, although they can be a helpful way to understand other people's general philosophies.

Introducing the parents

The parents I interviewed come from varied backgrounds. They include a social worker, several teachers, a speech therapist and an artist. Some studied to postgraduate level and some left school at 16. Two are single parents and the rest live with their partners. To make this lifestyle shift possible, some reduced their working hours or gave up work, and others combine accompanying their children with working part-time from home or tag-teaming with the other parent. Some have made big changes to their lives so they can make ends meet on a reduced income, including moving to be nearer to family and downsizing the family home. Two have another child who does attend school. Just one of the children has never attended school. The rest of the parents took their children out of school, either due to mental health concerns or because their children were unhappy or requested not to go to school any more. The children are aged 6 to 25, and several have a diagnosis of autism and/or ADHD. The four young people who are no longer school-aged are working or in higher education.

Holly
Sons, aged 10 and 6, and a daughter, aged 8.
Out of school for four years.

Holly chose to take her oldest son out of school when he was six. He had enjoyed Reception but became anxious and withdrawn in Year 1. When she saw how happy and relaxed he was at home during Covid-19, she decided not to take him back to school. Holly's middle child, her daughter, is autistic and was in nursery school at the time. Her younger son has never been to school.

> My eldest was fine in Reception but in Year 1, when the academics started, he complained about it a lot. He was sad and counting down days 'til the weekend, and having a lot of anxiety before bed if it was a school day the next day. He stopped going to the toilet at school because he didn't like the noises or crowds of people, so he would hold it in all day. He was just losing his spark, and saying things like 'I hate learning'. He was associating learning with writing stuff down. When I tried to explain that everything he was doing was learning, he couldn't get his head around that, because as far as he was concerned, he was being pulled away from the fun activities to do learning. And I thought there had to be a better way. Covid forced my hand, which I'm grateful for."

Eva
Sons, aged 13 and 10. Out of school for five years.

Eva's elder son Max attended a small village school until the age of eight, but found the pace difficult and stressful. Her younger son attended school for just a few days. Eva had thought about home educating when her children were younger, and eventually decided to try it when she saw how they were not naturally thriving within the school system.

> Max found the pace of school and the constant changing of subjects difficult. He really likes to properly grasp things at a deeper level, and just as he was getting into something, they'd change subject. It meant he didn't always get his work done in class. He was very average and he went unnoticed. The things that were celebrated in him were being cooperative and compliant."

Claire
Sons, aged 16 and 14. Out of school for five years.

Claire's sons were 11 and 9 when they left school. Her elder son found school challenging, and they tried three different schools to try to find one that was a good fit. The tipping point came when he began secondary school and his mental health plummeted. Claire felt she had no choice but to do something different. Her younger son coped with school, but was happy to leave.

> The school environment did not suit S. The situation had got so bad and I'd seen his mental health decline so much that I didn't really feel like there was a choice at that point. His whole spark had gone – the happy-go-lucky little boy wasn't there anymore. He was masking a lot. When he came home, he was exhausted, and that's when we had the big blow-ups. When we chose to leave school, friends and family kept saying, 'Gosh, you're so brave', and everyone was quite shocked. I suppose they saw it as a huge risk, but I just didn't see it that way at all. The brave thing would have been to leave him there."

Jayne
**Daughter, aged 10, and son, aged 8.
Out of school for two years.**

Jayne and her family decided to try home education when their daughter was eight. She had found school and Covid-19 overwhelming and became increasingly anxious. The family had taken a few months to go travelling, and seen such a change in their children that they realized they needed to give it some more time.

> Our daughter was in school until Year 3. She had a good start but she's very sensitive and quite a perfectionist. After Covid she started to struggle more and didn't want to get up in the morning or go to school. She was doing well academically but she was so anxious and overwhelmed. She would worry a lot about making mistakes and getting things wrong, and compare herself a lot to older children. She was really tying herself up in knots about how she should be. We eventually took the plunge a couple of years ago. Initially we just went travelling for a few months, but we saw such a difference in both our children – especially our eldest – that we knew we needed to give it at least a year."

Nicola
Son, aged 21, and daughter, aged 18. Out of school for 11 years.

Nicola took her children out of school when they were aged 7 and 10. A combination of life circumstances, including her cancer diagnosis and her son's serious illness, led her to make different life choices.

> When my children were three and six years old, I started to question why they were constantly ill. It occurred to me that they were chronically stressed. The way that I parented was not reflected in their daily school environment. At home we explored, coloured outside all of the lines and lived creatively. They were baffled by the contrast of their home life to the rigidity of their school life, and it showed. It took my own cancer diagnosis and the subsequent near-death illness of my

son for me to understand that childhood is not to be endured until formal education is over, and that they could pursue a life they loved."

Hayley
Daughters, aged 25, 22 and 11, and son, aged 18. Out of school for 14 years.

Hayley's older children were 9 and 11 when they left school. The younger two have never been to school. They decided to try home education at the request of her then 11-year-old daughter, who had always done well academically, but had never enjoyed school.

> It was a really positive choice in the sense that it wasn't because we thought everything was terrible at school so let's find an alternative. I was on the PTA [Parent Teacher Association] and was a school governor at both the primary and secondary school in our village. At the time I was working at a college and I was looking for some ideas for my class of 16- to 17-year-olds who were very disillusioned and I was trying to get them to engage. And for some reason, the internet delivered me a podcast about unschooling. My eldest daughter and I were listening to it in the car, and she was like 'What, you don't have to go to school?' So we looked up the local council's policy and it seemed really positive, then we both did loads of research and thought it was amazing. She'd never really enjoyed school, but she'd fitted in to a degree, and always got fantastic reports. So I thought, let's just try it, and we can always just do it for a year."

Rhonda
Stepdaughter, aged 15, and daughter, aged 13. Out of school for two years.

Rhonda's younger daughter left school when she was 11 after two years during which she had struggled to attend classes due to severe anxiety. Rhonda's stepdaughter is still at the same school.

> "I loved school. I was the PTA mum and always volunteering. But my daughter struggled and was always getting sent home with stomach aches and headaches. We put it down to separation anxiety because of the difficulties we had getting her into school. Every morning she would cry, but we got used to it, and the narrative was always that it was about us and not about school. Just before lockdown, we moved and she changed schools. After lockdown, she couldn't cope when she went back. We thought we had no option so we forced her to go to school. Finally, my husband took her one day in the car, and she screamed the whole way. When they got to school, a teaching assistant dragged her off him. We were both in tears that day and we decided we were never doing that again."

Donna
Daughters, aged 14 and 12. Out of school for three years.

Donna's elder daughter who is diagnosed autistic with pathological demand avoidance (PDA) traits, always found school extremely difficult. After many years of trying to make it work, her daughter's mental health was so bad that Donna realized she had no choice but to try something else. Donna's younger daughter is still at school.

> "Right from the beginning, my eldest didn't enjoy nursery. Then she went to a small village school, and after the first year, which was okay, she found it really challenging. Getting her to school became really difficult, but I just couldn't see any other possibility. We'd have hours of upset in the mornings, then she'd manage to contain herself at school, then come home and fall apart. We battled on through that for years. Covid happened when she was around nine and, without the stress of school, it was really amazing. She then went to secondary school and managed for three days, and it became obvious that she wasn't going to cope. At that point, the penny dropped, and I thought, there has to be another way."

Lianne
Daughter, aged 15. Never attended school.

Lianne's daughter tried nursery school but never attended primary or secondary school. Lianne and her partner were looking for alternatives to mainstream school, fuelled by their own experiences of school and the learning Lianne was doing when her daughter was a baby and toddler.

> Certain books, such as *The Continuum Concept* [by Jean Liedloff], had a profound impact on me. They made me question why we do what we do and the assumptions we have in the West that this is just the way it is. We'd been thinking of looking for an alternative school and we were figuring out how we could afford that. I'd never heard of unschooling until it came up in a conversation with someone, and this whole world just opened up."

Annie
Two sons, aged 8 and 7. Out of school for one year.

Annie took her sons out of school when they were six and seven. They had initially tried flexi-schooling, which had worked well, but then had to go for four days a week. Both boys became anxious and irritable, and getting them out of the house to go to school became increasingly difficult.

> It was clear that the boys were tired and irritable when I picked them up from school. Jack, who was seven at the time, became withdrawn, and Teddy started to worry about SATs [Standard Assessment Tests] and being tested. He was just six. He was also so anxious about reading as he'd been told in school that he should know more phonics for his age group. As a result, he simply shut down and refused to do any reading with me because he was 'stupid' and would 'never get it'. Getting them out of the house to attend school became a daily struggle. The final straw came with the arrival of the new Year 3 teacher who told me that her behavioural policy was 'scary', and

that if the children were good they would be rewarded with 'golden time' and stickers. It was then that we decided our children would not be returning to school for the new academic year, and our home ed journey began."

How to use this book

If unschooling feels too radical for you in the place you are in right now, I would invite you to keep going with all the things that are working in your home and to use the tools in this book to delve deeper into the things that create resistance or conflict. As you gain confidence and knowledge, you may find that you would naturally like to explore a little more.

Of course, there is privilege in being in a position to make major adjustments to our lives. If you are not able to make a shift now, whether due to your economic situation, your health, opposition from a partner or other family members, or for any other reason, then I hope this book is still helpful for you, and that it will give you useful tools to continue being your child's ally and advocate in learning and in life.

And finally, this book is not about whether home is better than school. Just as it is possible to create learning spaces for children in which they have agency to learn and thrive, so we can easily create a home environment in which they don't. While we certainly do need to revisit our beliefs around learning – and in our society these are heavily influenced by school – the best thing we can do is move away from the dichotomy of school vs. home and instead just keep asking the simple question, 'What do children need to thrive and learn?'

Good luck, and I hope that this book will be a helpful and reassuring companion on your journey.

❝ Once we decided to leave school, I thought, well, I'll just do school at home. Because I was a teacher, that's all I could imagine. But it just felt ridiculous and really forced and unnatural. My eldest is very compliant so he went along with a lot of this, but my youngest just threw it all back in my face. Then I heard this word 'unschooling' from someone who was unschooled as a child and, as soon as I read about it, I thought this makes so much sense. I thought we could give it a try while they're little and just see how it goes. And then his light came back and the fog lifted." HOLLY

Part 1

Learning about learning

Many parents assume that in order to help their children learn they need to recreate something that looks like school at home. In Part 1 we're going to see why this doesn't need to be the case at all, and how it might all look instead. We'll look at how natural learning takes place, and why it is inextricably linked to your child's sense of self, their values and their unique way of being, helping you to be far better prepared to support your child, not just in their learning, but in every aspect of their lives.

Chapter 1

How do children learn?

What is learning and what does it look like? Most of us automatically think of school when we think about learning. In fact, school is such an integral part of our culture that there seems to be little curiosity about how learning might unfold in any other way. Scores of research articles are published every year on how children learn best, and the vast majority are conducted in mainstream classrooms. Consequently, many of us assume that school and learning are pretty much the same thing, and conclude that the idiosyncrasies of school are essential for the intricate process of learning to take place in a child's brain.

In this context, it's no wonder parents feel nervous when they consider leaving mainstream education, and they wonder how they can recreate that same learning at home. Other people are genuinely mystified by the idea that this could look any other way. 'But how will they learn?' is a question you're likely to hear a lot in the beginning.

Even if you suspect there may be more to learning than school, you probably have lots of unconscious beliefs about how it should all look, particularly in the likely case that you went to school yourself. Many parents find that these beliefs have a surprisingly strong hold over them and cause endless worry and fear. Despite my own convictions that mainstream school was not the best fit for our children, it still took me quite a while to let go of maths workbooks and not fret about reading, writing, spelling or what would happen when they reached secondary school age. I was tested daily by the enormous gap between how I thought learning should look and how it actually looked.

If you are like me, and most parents I've spoken to, over time, and as you watch your child learning in ways you would never have imagined, you'll gradually lose these school-based beliefs and appreciate learning in a whole new light. You'll move right beyond notions of failure and success, and right and wrong, and eventually land in a far more satisfying, nuanced and joyful space. But being aware of your conditioned beliefs about learning right from the start can save you from a lot of frustration, arguments and sleepless nights. So, to really enjoy accompanying your child in their learning and to help them thrive, it's important to understand exactly what learning is and how it takes place.

Take a look at this list and see which of these common assumptions about learning feel familiar to you:

- Children need to focus on learning for several hours a day.
- Learning requires adult supervision and direction.
- Learning can be divided easily into different subjects.
- Successful learning requires reaching specific goals and outcomes.
- Children learn best with other children their own age.
- Learning is often difficult and sometimes boring or unpleasant.
- Adults have to work hard to motivate children to learn.
- A curriculum is essential to know what needs to be learned.

These are features of just about every school in the Western world and are based on the thinking that effective learning must be highly organized, focused and adult-directed. They double down on the idea that learning is hard work and requires immense effort and discipline on the part of the student. Learning may not be a lot of fun, but to have a successful life, a child must buckle down and push their way through regardless.

Our own school experiences are highly likely to back this all up. If we found school academically challenging, we may have assumed that learning was difficult or that we just weren't clever enough.

If we found school easy, we would have still been aware of all the children who struggled and were assigned to the lower sets. And there's plenty of proof from school itself that learning is difficult. Standardized testing is seen as a necessary evil from an early age to ensure that no one is falling behind and, as children get older, evenings and weekends are filled with homework. The overriding feeling is that there is a lot of information to assimilate within a short window of time. And to pile the stress on further, children are made to understand that success in all this is essential if they are to have any chance at a decent future.

So yes, if we look at learning through the lens of traditional school, it looks like hard work. And given the discipline required to be successful, it follows that many children need a lot of pushing and cajoling to get through it. There is the carrot, in the form of praise, good grades, prizes and good reports home, and there is the stick, in the form of bad grades, detentions, criticism and shame. The system perpetuates the widely-held belief that many children are intrinsically lazy. I have heard many parents say that their child 'would never learn anything if they weren't made to'. It is a sadly pessimistic but widespread view of children.

But what if this premise – that children must be pushed to learn – has little to do with the science of learning and with how humans are naturally wired to learn? What if the children who don't do well at school are not lazy and don't lack focus or discipline? What if the system simply fails to harness their natural motivation to learn, or, worse still, quashes the learning?

We will see now that much of what neuroscience has taught us about how learning happens in the brain, and the kind of environment that facilitates learning, runs directly counter to the ways the education system generally works. Many of the school-based assumptions we hold about learning have far more to do with the peculiarities of managing a system than with the way children learn.

Born to learn

School, as we know it in the Western world, has been around for a little more than 200 years. Modern humans, on the other hand, have been around for roughly 300,000 years. We can assume, then, that learning is as old as humankind or we would have died out long ago. But how does a human being take in new information, and how do we do this best? What we now call unschooling has long been a natural way of life for indigenous and hunter-gatherer communities.

Research published in 2023 by Dr Nikhil Chaudhary, an evolutionary anthropologist in the University of Cambridge's Department of Archaeology,[1] and Dr Annie Swanepoel, a child psychiatrist in Elysium Healthcare,[2] into indigenous and hunter-gatherer children shows that none of those Western school-based assumptions are considered necessary for learning in these cultures: 'they learn from one another, acquiring skills and knowledge collaboratively via play practice and exploration... Fundamentally, among hunter-gatherers, learning and play are two sides of the same coin' (Chaudhary and Swanepoel 2023, p.1524).

Direct teaching by adults is rare in these groups. Instead, children learn by engaging with life, learning from each other and from adults as they play and explore. For much of their days, they are in mixed-age groups and without adult supervision. Dr Chaudhary and Dr Swanepoel note that, 'Classroom schooling is often at odds with the modes of learning typical of human evolutionary history.' (Chaudhary and Swanepoel 2023, p.1524).

Of course, few of us live in small, intergenerational communities where our children are free to safely explore with other children. But even though the circumstances in which these communities live are certainly vastly different to our own – and have their own distinct challenges – Dr Chaudhary and Dr Swanepoel's research can still provide some insight into the importance of free play, independence and exploration in our children's development and learning.

---

1   www.arch.cam.ac.uk/staff/dr-nikhil-chaudhary
2   www.elysiumhealthcare.co.uk

Research in neuroscience backs up this idea that natural learning is active and exploratory, and that our brains are wired to learn through direct and meaningful experience. Since the mid-20th century, when the idea of neuroplasticity became widely understood, we have known that our brains continue to change throughout our lives according to the stimuli we receive, the experiences we have, and how we interpret these. As we move through life, encountering new information and situations, new connections – synapses – are created between neurons, and existing neural pathways are made stronger or weaker according to what we come across and its use to us. This process is at its most intense in babies and young children, whose brains are creating over a million new neural connections every second. As we get older, the forming of new synapses continues, but at a slower rate.

Neuroplasticity ensures that we can adapt to the ever-changing circumstances of our lives, acquiring the appropriate new skills and knowledge we need to get through life safely. So, from an evolutionary perspective, learning is not an extra thing we can choose to do or not do. Learning is an essential and integral part of our lives, and key to our survival. We simply can't not learn.

This doesn't mean that our brains deal with everything we experience equally. As well as constantly figuring out what new information we need to seek out, we are also sorting out which of the millions of pieces of information that we discover or that come our way we should retain. Because our lives are shaped by the knowledge and skills we acquire, we are far more likely to retain information that connects up with other things we already know, and that is relevant to our own lived experience, our sense of purpose and our future desires.

Dr Mary Helen Immordino-Yang, a professor of education, psychology and neuroscience at the University of Southern California, and author of *Emotions, Learning, and the Brain* (2015), has studied the link between emotions and learning for many years. Dr Immordino-Yang discusses the ideal biological conditions for learning, and how we are designed to learn about what matters to us. 'It is literally neurobiologically impossible to think deeply about things that you don't care about', she says (Lahey 2016). As adults, we know this.

We know that deep learning requires genuine engagement, and that engagement comes from meaning and purpose. When I ran my own business in Spain, I readily learned about Spanish employment and tax laws. I took courses in accounting, became proficient enough in all the computer programs I needed, and willingly acquired all the Spanish vocabulary necessary for my specific business. I recognized what I needed, and was happy to spend my time on things that, in another context, I would have run a mile from.

At secondary school, I was a keen student in language classes because I wanted to travel and was sure that French and Spanish would be relevant to my future, whereas in chemistry classes, try as I might, I seemed to have no way to grasp on to the knowledge. For all my staring at the whiteboard, there appeared to be nothing in my brain for the information to hook on to. I was relieved to discover that my brain was not at fault in those chemistry lessons. In fact, we could say that it was working optimally. In the words of Dr Immordino-Yang, 'Why would you waste time spending energy and effort and neurological resources on thinking about random things that don't have any bearing on anything important? That would be a silly use of energy' (Lahey 2016). Just to clarify, I don't think chemistry is not important, but my brain at that time and in that context did not consider it relevant for me, so it naturally struggled to engage. I am sure there are plenty of people who have had a similar experience in French or Spanish classes.

The power of intrinsic motivation

When we learn things because they are deeply meaningful or relevant to us, we don't need rewards or punishments. Our reward is the learning itself. Our prize is for our curiosity to be satisfied, and for our explorations to lead to discoveries. This is the power of intrinsic motivation.

We see this with babies and young children before they reach school age. We don't need to cajole them into anything, because their innate drive to learn and explore is unstoppable. Young babies spend much of their time awake observing and exploring with their hands, eyes and mouth. We know when they are getting ready to walk because they start to crawl and shuffle and lift themselves to their feet at every opportunity. We know that they are busy learning to talk by the sounds they make and copy for some time before real words come out. Learning to walk and talk are major accomplishments, but we have little to do with either, beyond providing a safe and loving environment within which they can freely experiment and explore. We can offer a helping hand with our child's first steps and celebrate their first words, but we don't need to offer prizes or rewards to motivate them. We know it would be a waste of time to try to control the process by giving them detailed instructions on how to walk or by insisting they practise specific words for a certain amount of time each day. We know that the impulse and timing have to come directly from them. And when they can walk, we toddler-proof our houses. Why? Because young children are intrinsically curious about life and want to learn everything they can about their environment.

Our own internal reward system

Because learning what we need to know is essential to our survival, we are wired to find it enjoyable and satisfying. In evolutionary terms, following our innate curiosity is the equivalent of giving ourselves the best chance at a long, healthy, happy life. In fact, when we attend to our inner desires to learn new skills and take on new challenges, we get a hit of dopamine, our body's way of letting us know that we're on a path that is right for us.

Interestingly, when we are driven by intrinsic motivation, rewards can be detrimental to our motivation. I used to be surprised that it didn't naturally follow that my children would want to take part in something competitive when they excelled at some sport or hobby. Who wouldn't be motivated by a prize? But research shows, as did my children, that offering a reward can have the opposite effect. Countless studies have shown this to be true in people of all ages (see, for example, Cameron and Pierce 1994; Deci, Koestner and Ryan 2001). By introducing an external reward, the focus shifts away from the activity itself to the goal, reducing the person's engagement in the activity. The reward also introduces the possibility of failure or of doing it wrong, along with the sense that someone else is now in control. And, as we'll see in a moment, none of us really like our journeys to be hijacked by others (Di Domenico and Ryan 2017).

Within a school environment, that dopamine hit rarely comes from exploring the world in the way that feels most meaningful to the child. There may be times that this is the case, such as an inspiring friendship or teacher, or a subject that a child naturally loves and is driven to understand more about. But generally, in a system based on carrots and sticks, the child must learn to get their dopamine hit from the satisfaction of external factors such as praise and good grades, rather than from their own motivation and sense of purpose. Tests and exams are certainly effective at getting students emotionally invested in learning specific material, particularly when we tell them that the consequences of failing are sure to be felt for the rest of their lives. But the emotional attachment is often to the outcome and not to the learning itself. By focusing so heavily on goals, we can be drawing children away from deep, meaningful learning. A teacher friend shared her frustration with me that whenever she goes off-curriculum and introduces wider material to her class, hands invariably shoot up with the question, 'Is this on the exam?'

A learning frame of mind

For deep learning to take place, we not only have to be emotionally invested in the learning itself (rather than in an externally created outcome), but we also have to be in the right frame of mind. We return once more to our evolutionary selves, whose top priority is survival at all costs. We are well-designed creatures, and until our health and safety are guaranteed, we can't turn our attention to learning. When we are stressed or anxious, our mammal brains are driven to take care of whatever urgent problem or threat is at hand. In this frame of mind, there is no room for intellectual curiosity, creativity or deep thinking – and extrinsic motivation tends to come with a layer of stress. It typically holds the weight of other people's expectations and the knowledge that we will be judged. It may motivate us to do what we're asked to do in our quest to be successful or to please, but it is also likely to engage our fear system (fight-or-flight) as we face the possibility of failure or shame. And, as we'll see later on, our autonomy is precious to us. No matter how compliant we are, none of us really wants someone else to call the shots in our lives. Simply put, when we attempt to motivate a child through fear or stress, we are unwittingly creating conditions that increase their resistance to learning.

On the opposite end of the spectrum is a learning frame of mind. Here, the child feels physically and emotionally safe and their nervous system is relaxed. Without external stress, the risk of failure or the need to focus on a specific goal, they feel neither rushed nor coerced. They are free to be open and curious, and can engage deeply with their ideas without worrying about what is right or wrong. In this frame of mind, learning is playful and exploratory, and all sorts of creative possibilities can take root and flourish.

I'm reminded of a podcast episode I recorded. My guest had worked as a teacher for many years, and she taught part-time in a high school when her children were young. She described the moment when she realized how different these two approaches to learning were. Her six-year-old son loved outer space and devoured everything he could on the topic. Together, they were reading books and doing research, and he had become quite an expert. At the same time, she was teaching space to her class of 12-year-olds because it was on the school curriculum. No matter what she did and what materials she used, she could not spark interest in these children. They had no control over their own learning, and the topic of space was, for now at least, not something any of them were keen to master. And although the teacher tried to create a supportive environment, no one could escape the fact that the learning was tied up in grades and expectations. My guest was taken aback by how, in her son's case, the learning was playful and flowed easily, whereas at school it felt difficult and resistant. The stark difference in the children's experience of the same subject was a clear reminder of how important autonomy is for children in their learning.

Learning and playfulness

Perhaps one of the most misleading assumptions we have all picked up from school is that learning is serious and play is fun. I remember myself, coming home from school in the 1970s, changing out of my school uniform and heading straight out to play with other children on our street. Play could not have looked or felt more different from learning. Different place, different time of day, different (mixed-aged) children, different clothes, no adults, no specific goals, and lots of freedom.

Newly home-educating parents often worry that their children aren't learning anything because all they want to do is play. They might be delighted that their children are happy and enjoying themselves, but since we all associate learning with the hard work of school, their children's play looks too much like fun to have any real value. It might be enjoyable, says adult logic, but it won't get them anywhere. At some point children surely must get on with the difficult task of learning.

But, just as living and learning cannot be pulled apart, neither can play and learning. Peter Gray, author and a research professor at Boston College,[1] has spent many years studying the interconnecting nature of play and learning. He makes the point that children are biologically designed to learn what they need in order to become effective adults in the culture into which they are born, and that this process naturally involves play. Gray makes a powerful case for the need for independent play in his book, *Free to Learn*: 'We have forgotten that children are designed by nature to learn through self-directed play and exploration, and so, more and more, we deprive them of freedom to learn, subjecting them instead to the tedious and painfully slow learning methods devised by those who run the schools' (Gray 2013, p.65).

---

[1] www.petergray.org

When my children were small, they created a number of complex games together, one of which they played for several years. This game involved numerous toys, each with their own backstory, personality and voice. These characters were engaged in ongoing plots and subplots, with rules and relationships that I struggled to grasp. The three of them would retire to one room for this game, and the rest of the house would fall quiet for hours on end. I might hear occasional laughter, but mostly I'd just hear the voices of the different characters, punctuated by the odd discussion of what should happen next. Arguments during this game were rare. If ever anyone decided to quit because they disagreed with something, the other players would look for a compromise, and usually come up with some ingenious plot twist that kept everyone happy. I would pop in sporadically to offer food and drink and often find three solemn faces looking back at me. They would wait patiently for me to deliver their snack or do whatever I was doing, before asking me to close the door behind me and resuming their game. Although at that point I don't think I quite understood the value of their play, there was never any doubt that it was serious stuff.

Play (unless an adult decides to take over) is intrinsically motivated and deeply meaningful to the child who is playing. Through imaginary play, children explore and reenact ideas from the adult world; they solve problems, create rules and work together. Not only that, but this relaxed, open and curious frame of mind is ideal for absorbing new information.

Play will almost certainly be a large part of your child's learning journey, and perhaps one of your first tasks is to really learn to value and appreciate play in whatever form it takes for your child. Keep reminding yourself that it is not the opposite of learning but a fantastic vehicle for natural, meaningful learning. And watching your child play will give you a valuable insight into what they like to engage with and how. You are also going to quickly realize that this is all about so much more than learning. As we'll see in the next chapter, learning is a key part of a far bigger quest – children understanding themselves and who they are in the world.

But if they don't do well at school…

Can a child do well in life if they don't do well at school? This question can pose a dilemma for a parent whose child is struggling at school. While wanting to take them out of a place where they are not thriving, they also worry they may potentially damage their child's chances of success in life. This is a powerful narrative in our society. Why else would we turn somersaults to get our children into 'good' schools, drag distressed children in when they don't want to go and think it's acceptable for young people to get deeply stressed about exams? Surely because in the long term, doing well at school is worth all the sacrifices, including mental health challenges.

This is a tricky narrative to unpick because while it does contain some truth, it is also misleading. On the one hand, good academic results certainly open doors. If you want to go to university as a young person, you'll probably need to have taken some exams (although there can be alternative routes), and many jobs require specific qualifications. It is also true that within the school system, a child who struggles, can't focus or has low attendance is likely to be less academically successful, and so some of those doors won't be so readily open to them.

But let's dig a little deeper. The thing about taking school out of the equation completely is that you remove this fundamental idea of a child doing well or badly. When we stop comparing and judging, we can appreciate that every child has the potential to do brilliantly, not just at school, but at life. Creativity, innovation and out-of-the-box thinking come naturally to children. Those who are naturally academic will seek out knowledge in the areas that light them up, and be drawn to a path that uses their skills. In the UK, there are many ways for a child to access qualifications outside of the school structure. Some take enough GCSEs to get a place at sixth form college, and others might pace themselves and take a couple of GCSEs a year over a few years. They might study by themselves at home, join in-person or online study groups or any combination of those. Maybe they'll take longer than their peers, or maybe not. These children are likely to have many other things that they love to learn about and that are fulfilling to them. So, while doing well in their exams may be important to them, their sense of worth is far less likely to be tangled up in their results.

And for children whose paths are less academic, being out of a system that values academia above all else gives them the freedom to embrace and value their particular skills and interests. Rather than internalizing any sense of not being enough or failing, they turn their focus to the things they are naturally drawn to, with their sense of self intact. If exams need to be taken at any point to reach the next part of their journey, the intrinsic motivation they are used to tapping into will serve them far better on their journey than fear of failure.

We might also want to question how we measure success. Many of my podcast guests are parents who did well at school. They worked hard and followed a straight path to university. But a common thread is the regret that they never really knew what their passions were, or had the time to delve deep into things that were not needed on that straight path. Many felt that following the rules, conforming and getting the grades were so highly valued and entrenched in them that later on they were often unable to work out the best choices for themselves. And, as the late Sir Ken Robinson pointed out in his famous TED talk,[1] conforming and following rules may have been helpful lessons for the children of newly industrialized nations, but maybe not so much for those coming of age in the 21st century, where creativity, innovation and out-of-the-box thinking are highly prized.

Unsurprisingly, there are few studies on how children who grow up without school fare as adults. However, the little research that does exist points to the notion that children can

[1] www.ted.com/talks/sir_ken_robinson_do_schools_kill_creativity?subtitle=en

fare well without school. In 2015 in the US, Peter Gray published the results of his study of 75 adult unschoolers (Gray and Riley 2015). Of these, 83 per cent had gone on to some form of higher education, and 44 per cent had completed a Bachelor's degree or higher, or were currently full-time students in a Bachelor's programme: 'The great majority of respondents who went on to college reported no difficulty doing the academic work. Indeed, most said they were at an academic advantage, primarily because of their high motivation and their high capacity for self-initiative, self-direction, and self-control' (Gray 2013). There are obvious limits to the study, but there are interesting themes that run through the responses. Those who did not go to college or university intentionally chose different paths that they were happy with, including a high number of entrepreneurs and people in creative careers.

So, can your child do well in life if they don't have the opportunity to do well in school? Yes, absolutely. The journey will certainly look different and it may not be such a straight line through, but it will be meaningful to them, aligned with who they are, and reach far beyond the limits of any curriculum.

Journal prompts

- What assumptions around learning do you think you'll find challenging to let go of?

- Think about your deepest learning experiences as an adult. How did these unfold, and why were they meaningful to you?

- Observe your child as they play. Can you see what is meaningful and engaging to them?

Chapter summary

- Most of us are brought up to see school as synonymous with learning, leading to the belief that structured, adult-led teaching is the only way for children to learn.

- Research shows that from birth, children are naturally driven to learn through meaningful engagement with life. An intrinsically motivated child engages in the learning – not for external goals, but for the satisfaction of the learning itself.

- A learning frame of mind is relaxed and curious, whereas a child who is anxious or stressed is naturally less open to learning.

- Learning happens naturally through play. Play allows children to explore, solve problems and create meaning in a relaxed, enjoyable and stress-free way.

Chapter 2

Learning to be themselves

Some years ago, I asked one of my children what they thought about the term 'unschooling'. They took a moment to mull it over and then answered that they didn't like it because it had nothing to do with school. I asked what word they would use instead and they said, 'I'd probably just call it "living".' And they're right – learning is not separate from the rest of life. It is naturally woven into every aspect of our children's lives. And since living and learning are so deeply entwined, in this chapter we're going to look at how the way our children live is key to both their learning and their happiness.

When I ask parents to think about what they want for their children, few of the answers have anything to do with academics and everything to do with leading a happy and fulfilling life. They want their children to grow into emotionally competent adults who know how to navigate the ups and downs of life without getting overwhelmed. They want them to recognize and value their natural gifts, choose healthy relationships and be able to stand up for themselves. Above all, they want their children to feel good about being themselves. For many of these parents, the reason for leaving the education system had nothing to do with learning and everything to do with their child's sense of wholeness.

Living life in all its fullness

Learning beyond school allows us to create an environment in which our children can acquire deep self-knowledge about what they need to thrive and learn in the world. They can live fully into who they are and become knowledgeable about their own unique needs and desires. They can have the space to explore life at their own pace and according to their own values, guided by the things that interest them and that make them feel curious. No longer under pressure to meet other people's expectations, or being rushed from one adult-directed activity to another, a new space can open up, both mentally and physically. Here, they can figure out why something does or doesn't feel good, what direction a new interest needs to take, or why a social group they enjoyed last week no longer holds appeal. When there is no sense of blame or failure, even the most difficult situations can be held with curiosity and compassion. Living and learning in this way is no longer about preparing for being an adult. It is about living life right now, in all its fullness.

So how can we support our children in their lives and their learning so they can show up fully as themselves?

Our child's internal navigation system

We all have an internal navigation system that works hard to keep us connected to our sense of self and to our values. This is that same system that drives us to embark on learning journeys – not to please someone else, but just because we feel compelled to. And this is the system that rewards us with a gratifying sense of satisfaction when we find the places, people and activities that are aligned with our values and interests. When a child is connected to their navigation system, they have a keen sense of who they are and they know when something feels right for them and when it doesn't. They know what wholeness feels like.

Having the confidence and insight to stay connected to their navigation system in a society that values external rewards and compliance so highly can be tricky. As we saw in the previous chapter, the extrinsically rewarding nature of school and general beliefs about how children should behave mean that a child's sense of what is right for them is being constantly recalibrated to meet other people's expectations. Being accepted, fitting in, reaching someone else's goals and pleasing others are often the measures of success. So, rather than tapping into what matters to them, children are taught to place a higher value on what other people expect of them. At home, at school and in wider society, compliance in children is generally admired and rewarded. Our children learn which parts of themselves are pleasing to others and worthy of praise and which parts are best kept hidden. They quickly figure out who they should be, often at the expense of who they are.

How our childhood experiences affect us

The beliefs we acquire about ourselves as children, and the patterns we create around them, have profound ramifications for how we live our lives as adults. These childhood messages about how we need to show up become so deeply ingrained that it can soon become impossible to distinguish between what is external and what is internal. Typically this plays out in battles between what we want to do and what we feel we 'should' do. Many parents I speak to feel that they were considered successful as children but at a high cost to their sense of authenticity. The constant shapeshifting to get things right, to be liked, and to avoid shame or failure left them adrift and making choices that looked right on the outside but felt uncomfortable on the inside. Over the years and decades, they got so used to needing external validation and to measuring themselves against someone else's definition of success that they lost connection with their own compass.

Self-Determination Theory: driven by our need to grow and be fulfilled

Just as we are all born to learn, so we are all driven by the need to grow and feel fulfilled. This understanding is the premise of Self-Determination Theory, which was pioneered over 30 years ago by psychologists Edward Deci and Richard Ryan (Ryan and Deci 2000). Their research found that people perform better, and lead happier, more satisfying lives when living in alignment with their internal desires and choices rather than being driven by outside influences. The theory is based on the premise that we all have an innate need to create a cohesive sense of self and to continually improve and expand our knowledge. It's a helpful framework for understanding what our children need in order to thrive and how we can support them.

In order for our internal lives to flourish, we must have the right conditions. In particular, there are three essential psychological needs that must be met:

- Autonomy
- Competence
- Connection.

Autonomy

Knowing that we are in charge of our own lives is enormously important to humans, and we need autonomy like we need air. Without it, we are thwarted in the world, unable to experience new things in our own time, to pursue what is meaningful to us or even perhaps to keep ourselves safe. If you've ever felt trapped in a job, relationship or any other situation that seemed to have no way out, you might have felt the helplessness that comes when you can't seem to have an impact on your own circumstances. Feeling like we have no control over our lives is strongly linked to depression and anxiety. So, although compliant children are generally celebrated, and parents are taught to expect and demand compliance from their children, it's helpful to remember that not wanting to be controlled by others is also a natural and healthy aspect of being human. When a child resists being controlled or coerced, they are often labelled naughty or disrespectful, but they may well be protecting their extremely precious autonomy.

Why we don't trust children

Unfortunately, autonomy is the need that children are perhaps most routinely deprived of, often with the reasoning that it is for their own sake. We seem to be collectively terrified of children having any agency over their own lives, and the idea of children 'doing what they want' sets many adults on edge. One of the most obvious reasons for this is that we don't trust children to make good choices, so we feel the need to show them what good choices are. This adult logic assumes that by setting and enforcing clear rules and norms for children to live by, they will internalize them and ultimately live by them as adults. Make a child study something they don't like and they will learn that hard work and study are important. Make a child attend a social group against their will and they'll learn to make friends. Make a child do something they're scared of and they'll learn to be brave.

The problem with this way of thinking is that not only does it not work, but it directly opposes our children's need for autonomy. So, rather than setting them up for a healthy life, we inadvertently take away their agency and make them less resilient. Not only do we disempower them through coercion, but they don't learn the lesson we intend for them to learn at all. Instead, they learn that studying is boring and to be avoided at all costs, that they are strange and unusual for not wanting to go to a social group, or that we don't listen or keep them safe.

> I realized that, for my family, autonomy was the missing piece of the puzzle. I have a really strong need for autonomy and I probably always have done, but I didn't have the opportunity for autonomy as a child. This realization has impacted how I parent and in how I see our children. They are their own people, and we're all on an equal

plane. I think difficulties arose before because my children didn't feel like they had a voice. It doesn't always equal an easy life because there are always four opinions and they'll tell me when they don't want to do something. But I wouldn't change it at all. I don't want them to conform." CLAIRE

❝ In the first few months of deschooling, they had the space to recover from school and I found a lot of our conversations kept coming back to why they found school hard and a lot of this was to do with their lack of autonomy – restrictions on toilet time, eating their sandwiches first before other items in their lunchbox, being with children every day that they didn't particularly like, etc." ANNIE

Autonomy to take responsibility

In his book *Nonviolent Communication*, Marshall B. Rosenberg presents a compelling case for autonomy and against coercion. He sees the external imposition of someone else's will as creating superficial compliance that may tick a box but, since it is based on coercion, is essentially void of meaning. Rosenberg makes the point that unless we make our own choices, we don't take full responsibility for them: 'We are dangerous when we are not conscious of our responsibility for how we behave, think, and feel' (2015, p.16). So, not only does coercion never actually teach the intended lesson, but when children (and adults) do things because they 'have to', they understandably don't feel ownership of their actions. We've probably all had the frustrating experience of interacting with people who claimed to have no choice, agency or responsibility. A child who has the autonomy to make choices gets used to holding the weight of their own decisions.

Autonomy to practise making aligned choices

So what does this mean in our day-to-day lives with our children? It means that if we want to help them become familiar with how to make choices and decisions that feel aligned to them (in learning and in life) we have to learn to trust them. The biggest shift that most of us will make as we explore learning beyond school is letting go of the idea that it is always up to us to make the 'right' choices for our children. Instead, we need to encourage them to connect with their navigation system and figure out what feels right to them.

> My 11-year-old daughter was talking about her day. She's going through a highly planned phase. She likes to time-block her day and she's got these little tasks that she wants to work on. She's making a photo book and she wants to do so many minutes a day on it, and she has monthly goals of how many times she wants to go swimming and cycling and different things. She told me that she has a lot of practice at making decisions and she thinks that's good because it's helping her learn how to think about things and to be more thoughtful when she makes a decision. She thinks it has given her some valuable skills, like planning and taking responsibility." **HAYLEY**

> My daughter started a page for fans of female pop artists because she found that the ones that existed were mean and unpleasant. She decided how it would work, wrote the group guidelines and moderates the group. They share content they've created and it's a really kind and supportive space. What I've seen emerge from her when left to do what makes her happy is that she finds solutions and is a bit of a leader. And it's all purely her." **RHONDA**

Autonomy to choose what they learn

Learning from a place of autonomy is essential to your child's ever-evolving sense of self. When they have the autonomy to choose what they learn about, they will naturally gravitate to those things that are meaningful to them in some way and, as you watch your child explore new pursuits or dig deep into their interests, you'll notice how this self-driven learning lights them up. You may well see how their values are also tied up in what they delve into. I've seen a love of animals lead to vegetarianism, volunteering and an interest in animal rights. A passion for Ancient Rome and battle strategy, explored through books and gaming, has led easily to a wider interest in politics and leadership. A love of history first nurtured by *Horrible Histories* has taken many twists and turns and has also fed a desire to understand more about the way the world is now organized. An interest in maps has developed into the studying of lesser-known languages and cultures, and an interest in their preservation. All these interests also fuel conversations about the future and ideas for jobs, careers, travel and studies. And, of course, just as our children are always growing and learning, new activities and interests appear, aligned with who they are and where they are right now in their lives. I look back at what each child has chosen to learn and how they each create their own ever-evolving curriculum. Never in a million years could I have guessed what this curriculum would contain, much less have been able to prepare it for them.

> My oldest daughter said that although there were lots of distractions at university, she always felt like she was a little bit ahead of the others because she'd never been told that she had to do the work. She always did things because she wanted to. She had friends who just wouldn't get their work done and she'd ask them why. She could see that even though they liked the subject there was that resentment of being told what to do. They were sort of rebelling again. She felt it was easier for her because that's how she'd always worked anyway, and she was there out of choice. She knew that if she wanted, she could leave." HAYLEY

Autonomy to set their own boundaries and advocate for themselves

The term 'boundary' is often used in a parenting context to talk about setting limits for our children. But boundaries aren't a standard set of rules. We create them as we move through life and they change according to our state of mind, our circumstances and the people we are with. One person's boundaries will be entirely different from another person's and, importantly, they exist to keep us safe. We know when a boundary has been crossed because we feel it in our bodies. When this warning system works well and we are confident in our abilities to advocate for ourselves, we can take whatever action is needed. As adults, we know how hard it can be to understand or advocate for our boundaries because they often compete directly with social norms and expectations. Even though we feel uncomfortable about something, our desire to be liked and accepted or our fear of disapproval may lead us to say yes instead of no. Have you ever taken on extra obligations with a heavy heart or stayed silent even though you wanted to speak out? Have you ever said yes when you wanted to say no?

A huge benefit of learning beyond school is that we can help our children understand and advocate for their boundaries. For many children, advocating for themselves in a large class of peers, where there may be all sorts of complex social dynamics to figure out, is overwhelming. Out of school, they can have the space to develop and trust their boundaries, and we can support them in speaking up when they need to. And, by going at their own pace, they have the time to develop their own wisdom around people and environments. This could initially translate into a child choosing to only socialize with a small group of trusted people, having the freedom to leave places or activities that don't yet feel safe to them or speaking to us if they are uncomfortable about something. As their confidence in self-advocacy increases, they are likely to open up to new people and situations, and as they grow older and enter their teenage years and then adulthood, they will be far better equipped to recognize if a situation does not feel safe and to speak up or leave. The years of advocating for themselves and being listened to will serve them well.

And, of course, all this means being okay with our children saying no to us too. If we want them to know their boundaries and to advocate for themselves, we need to move beyond the commonly held view that a child must always do as they're told, and take them seriously when they don't agree with us. In fact, we need to let them practise with us. This can be uncomfortable for parents who are used to equating good parenting with never giving in. But, by valuing our children's voices we are giving them the message that they deserve to be heard and listened to, even if that makes the day a bit more complicated.

> My daughter knows who she is and what she wants to do, and she's not frightened to just be her, which is massive, because when she was in school, that was a huge issue. She was so consumed by what everybody else was doing that she found it really, really hard to find herself and find her own voice. And now she has her voice. I've seen a huge difference in both my children's ability to advocate for themselves and a drastic shift in emotional regulation. I would say that the way that we're living now, with that autonomy and ability to choose how they operate in environments, really makes a difference." JAYNE

> I often fall into the trap of assuming that I am the one suggesting the better activity. 'This is good for you, and what you want to do isn't good for you.' I sometimes just have to let her explain her reasons to me and then I think, actually that's really cool that you're saying no. You're clear about what you want and you're advocating for yourself." RHONDA

> Knowing yourself is so important and I don't think anyone is immune to modern-day pressures of who we're supposed to be. She knows she can trust her own judgement, and she's very clear about what she wants to do and who she wants to spend time with." LIANNE

Autonomy to follow their rhythms

I recently saw a post in an online forum where a mother felt bad for not allowing her 15-year-old daughter to take a day off school when she was feeling very tired. Her choice to send her daughter in was almost unanimously applauded by other members of the forum. Most respondents insisted that the daughter had to learn what responsibility looks like, and others suggested that if the mother gave an inch, her daughter would take a mile. One even said the request itself showed that the mother had failed in her duty to bring her 15-year-old up properly. And now it was too late, because look how badly she'd turned out.

I wonder why we are so harsh on our children. As adults, we preach self-care to exhausted parents, GP practices are filled with burnt-out employees, and we applaud people who leave the rat race and create a lifestyle that allows for rest. Which of these narratives do we believe? That we should learn how our own rhythms work and recognize when we are pushing too hard and need some downtime? Or that we should learn to push on regardless, because that is our obligation to society? It reminds me a little of being a new mother and feeling absolutely exhausted but still choosing my endless to-do list over having a nap. 'Have the nap!' I would like to scream at my younger self, but my younger self was unfortunately too conscientious to look after herself.

When a child has the autonomy to follow their own rhythm, they can honour their needs while also learning a lot about themselves. They learn what it feels like in their body when they don't get enough exercise or pack a day with too many things. They become familiar with what energizes them and what leaves them depleted. And they can learn to respect that most precious and guilt-inducing commodity – rest. Having autonomy means they can start from an early age to do what I did not yet know how to do as a young mother – work out how to balance the demands of life and other people alongside taking good care of themselves.

> I think they know themselves very well. They know when they're tired and they say things like, 'I'm just having a hard day, so I need to do this or that'. They've never been shamed for their feelings, and my hope is that they can hold on to themselves and always know what they need in the moment rather than pushing themselves. They have a lot of space to rest and a lot of space to reflect. Not being forced to do something is counter-cultural, but it's important to know when to rest without guilt or shame. We know as adults that we can learn skills when we need them. I learned to bake as an adult, I learned Swedish, and I learned how to drive. The content is easy. The hard bit is knowing yourself." HOLLY

> I've treasured her being on her own sleep rhythm. Even at 15, she's early to bed and early to rise, as that suits her." LIANNE

> **"** What I really see is that so many of us need to slow down. There's a natural rhythm we need to follow, but we don't so we get ill and stressed. In school you're on a train going very fast toward a destination, and the child doesn't know if they want that. At home you have the space and time to say, well let's look more into that." NICOLA

Autonomy to know when it's time to move on

We tend to assume that sticking at things is an all-round good thing, and associate it with all sorts of wonderful values, such as self-discipline, resilience and commitment. Giving up and quitting, on the other hand, are generally frowned upon as signs of weakness of character. So we insist that our children see things through to the bitter end, for fear that otherwise they will grow up weak-willed and unable to ever stick to anything. It's true that some things do take a little while to figure out, and if we gave things up in the first five minutes, we might never discover anything new. And, if you've invested time and money into something, there is some understandable frustration that can come with your child quitting.

However, knowing when it's time to move on is also a valuable thing to learn in life. Whether it's a relationship, a job, a living situation or a friendship, recognizing that it no longer works and having the confidence to move on is essential for a fulfilling life. Through practice, a child can acquire the subtle skill of working out these often more nuanced aspects of life.

Competence

When did you last learn a new skill? Whether it was putting up shelves, editing a video or learning Italian, remember how good it felt to finally figure it out? To go from feeling incompetent and confused to enjoying a sense of accomplishment and feeling more than a bit pleased with yourself? Alongside autonomy, to lead a happy and satisfying life we need to experience the feeling of competence. We all want and need to be good at things and enjoy the confidence boost that comes from mastering a skill. Learning new things reassures us that we can be effective and useful in the world. And children want to matter just as much as adults do.

And, of course, autonomy and intrinsic motivation are essential components of competency. Becoming good at what feels important to them is always going to be far more fulfilling for your child than becoming good at something because someone else says so. So, for our children to get the most out of becoming experts, we need to make sure that the following conditions are fulfilled.

Your child chooses what they want to master

When free to choose, your child will naturally seek to become competent in all sorts of areas. It could be dinosaurs, LEGO®, gaming, a musical instrument, football or history, for example. Many parents find it hard to understand why their child dedicates so much time to one particular subject or interest, particularly if they can't see the value in it. But if we step away from the subject itself, we'll see that these deep dives are how children explore their natural desire to feel competent and get to experience the joy of true competence.

> My son loves learning about Pokémon, and basically taught himself to read to be able to access this compendium of Pokémon. He knows most of the characters, their moves, how they operate within that world and how they interact with each other. He watches the programmes and he's got a couple of books that he looks at. I initially thought, 'Oh God! It's such a waste of time!', but I've realized that that's the way he learns things, and he has applied that to other things. We've listened to the Percy Jackson books, and he has been learning loads about the Greek gods and the Norse gods and the Roman gods and the Egyptian gods. And again, it's that sort of world building, putting information together and understanding how it all feeds into each other." JAYNE

Your child sets their own goals

To gain competence, we each need to go at our own pace. If the goal seems unrealistic or we get too far out of our depth, we easily feel deflated or frustrated, and as our sense of competency plummets, so does our motivation for the task. By setting their own goals and milestones, your child can get used to feeling into that sweet spot between aiming too high and getting demotivated, and aiming too low and not enjoying the satisfying buzz of doing something really well.

> She's gained a lot of confidence from doing the things she wants to do. She's so motivated to overcome obstacles, and that gives her confidence to believe she can make things happen. It's a valuable skill to know that if she wants something enough, she will find a way to achieve it. For example, she's now able to give college a try. At one point, she didn't think that was possible, but now she has learned that she can give things a go." DONNA

There should be no external sense of failure or success

Your child will know full well if they have lived up to their own challenge or not. And if they feel they haven't, they may well feel disappointment and frustration. This doesn't mean we don't commiserate if they need a shoulder to cry on or celebrate their victories with them when things go to plan. But, unless asked for by our child, we need to hold back from piling our own expectations on. As we'll see in later chapters, it can be surprisingly easy to add pressure without realizing it.

Connection

And finally, connection – to thrive and learn, our children must feel *safe* and *loved*. We saw in Chapter 1 how important a relaxed nervous system is for learning, and being accompanied by people who respect and appreciate them is also essential for a child's growing sense of self. Strong relationships that make them feel safe and valued give them the confidence to explore and venture out confidently in their own time.

As you read through this book, you'll see that your relationship with your child is the foundation on which everything else, including learning, is built. Ironically, it is often the parent's worry around learning that causes the most friction and arguments in the home, and it can easily undermine the relationship. However, as you deschool, you'll find that you naturally start to spot old patterns and conditioning that cause tension, and you'll learn to open up to new ways of responding. Over time, you'll see how all the little daily shifts you make strengthen your connection with your child. It has been fascinating to me how many parents have told me over the years that their deschooling has been a profoundly healing journey for them and their child. When a parent is no longer held hostage to all the 'shoulds', or needs their child to be a certain way for things to be okay, they are free to see and appreciate their child in their wholeness.

Your child will also have the freedom to choose how they engage and connect with other adults and children, enabling them to create connections that are valuable and supportive. When they don't need to worry about whether or not they fit into environments that don't feel right, they can seek out places and friendships where they truly belong.

Define your 'whys'

No matter how you arrived at the decision to home educate, it's important to acknowledge any conflicting feelings while also starting to reframe this new path in a positive way. If the road so far has been bumpy, there may well be a lot of healing that needs to happen – that will come in its own time, and far more easily if you are able to embrace this new way of life whole-heartedly.

You may understandably have had your focus on all the reasons that school hasn't worked or won't work for your child, and all the 'why nots' are probably taking up a lot of headspace. But it's time now to dive into all the 'whys' – all those reasons why this change can be a wonderful opportunity for your child and for your family.

Think about all the positive aspects of your child living and learning beyond school. These may have to do with mental health, learning, relationships in the family, lack of peer pressure or the freedom to be themselves. And what are the benefits for you and your relationship with your child? These might include having time to reconnect, having less external stress in your life, the freedom to plan some fun activities for you both, or just time to slow down and focus on recalibrating your nervous systems.

Write all these things down and check in with them often. Try reading through them as soon as you get up in the morning, holding the daily intention of seeing this as a new and exciting path. Whisk the list of 'whys' out when you feel overwhelmed or worried, and remind yourself of what is really important for your child. As you keep intentionally reframing this experience and letting go of all the things that have felt difficult and problematic, you'll start to appreciate all the positives that are present. And as you shift your perspective, you'll be able to start to build on those things. In Part 2 of this book you'll find lots of tools to help you through those difficult moments, and keep you and your child focused on all the 'whys'.

Journal prompts

- In what ways could you give your child more autonomy?
- What does your child like to do that gives them a feeling of competence?
- Do you think your child feels safe and connected? Are there ways that you could nurture your connection with them, or their connections with other people?

Chapter summary

- Living and learning are inseparable, and most parents want their children to be happy and to lead fulfilling lives. So how we approach learning is key to our children living in a way that feels coherent and authentic to them.

- We all have an internal navigation system that guides us, based on our values and interests. In a society that has so many external demands, it can be hard to stay connected, but we can support our children in staying connected to theirs.

- Self-Determination Theory is a helpful lens with which to consider what our children need to thrive. Autonomy is vital for personal growth, and allowing children to make their own choices fosters many personal values, including responsibility and resilience.

- All humans look for competence. We can give our children the right conditions for them to become experts in the things that interest them.

- Feeling safe and loved is essential for our children to learn and grow. Strong connections help our children feel valued and confident. And a relaxed nervous system is far more open to learning.

Chapter 3

What does self-directed learning look like in action?

It can be extremely challenging to accompany your child's learning at first because it looks so different from how you might have always considered learning to look. It's quite a leap of faith to go from something orderly and with a tangible output to a journey of exploration that's essentially being invented as it goes. If school-style learning is a series of straight lines, you might imagine self-directed learning as an intricate web of interconnected threads. Some of the threads keep weaving their way steadily through the weeks, months and years, whereas others might pop up, join a couple of dots together and then disappear, never to be seen again. Or they seem to be heading in one direction, and then veer off on a tangent to somewhere entirely different. And while it all makes perfect sense to the child, to the parent it can be both bewildering and endlessly fascinating.

'What do they do all day?', people will almost certainly ask you. In the beginning, you might feel a little defensive and find yourself listing all the activities and learning opportunities that arise, and all the ways that the learning is visible and quantifiable. Over time, and as you grow in confidence, you'll start to appreciate that these tangible things are part of a far richer context. You may still feel you need to give people something they can grasp onto, but you'll be aware that the richest and most meaningful parts of it all are difficult to put into words.

It's about the process, not the outcome

Always remember that whereas curriculum learning is about reaching a goal, when your child is self-directed, there's nothing more rewarding than the journey itself. Everything we talked about in the previous chapter, from learning about their rhythms to practising how to make aligned choices and advocating for themselves, is bound up in how they learn and what they choose to learn. There is so much self-knowledge to be gained by a child trying things out, being bored, deep diving into obscure subjects, taking a break when they need to and figuring out how they best acquire knowledge and expertise. When they forge their own path, they will be natural lifelong learners.

It sounds like a paradox, but when the goal is not a specific learning outcome, the learning comes far more easily. When we push children toward what we think is right, we not only create a natural resistance in them by overriding their autonomy, but we also interfere with the process of them figuring out the best next step themselves. So, when we let go of our idea of the perfect outcome, we are also empowering our children to understand how to live their own lives.

Let's see how this might all look in action and the key considerations to remember.

It's an open-ended exploration

One of the most important differences between self-directed learning and curriculum-based learning is that self-directed learning is an open-ended exploration. There are no limits for the child. For all of us whose main experience of learning comes from school, this is a potentially overwhelming thought. Instead of dedicating many hours a day to specific predetermined subjects, each containing a defined and finite amount of content to be learned in a particular order, the entire world and beyond is now our child's oyster. I have never met a self-directed child who chose to learn as a child would in school – covering each subject until just the right amount of knowledge had been learned, regardless of whether it was of interest to them or not. I have, however, met many children who have become incredibly knowledgeable and proficient in areas of interest to them. They have become experts in linguistics, space, maths, game design, horse care, horticulture or art, and often these have become the basis for their future studies and career choices. The lack of limits or prescribed goals means that they can pursue their interests far beyond what a curriculum allows for. Letting go of the boundaries of a fixed curriculum can certainly feel disorientating, but it's also exciting and allows for deeper, more expansive learning.

> Initially, we tried to do school at home and I tried lots of different things, but S wasn't really into it. I'd think about the subjects they'd enjoyed at school and suggest we did more of that. So although I was trying to do it in a less schooly way, they were still quite schooly things. Everything was instigated by me rather than by the children. All the time, I was thinking 'Where's the learning? What can I teach them? I have to teach you. We have to learn stuff!' At one point I realized it wasn't the children, it was me. That was the shift I needed. It took a long time, though – it wasn't overnight. My own education played a huge part here. I had a strong desire to get it right and to show people how good I am. So even when my perspective shifted, I was still putting so much pressure on it all." CLAIRE

The learning is not linear

In school, it is expected for there to be steady progress across the board, whereas at home this is unlikely to be the case. You may find that your child goes quickly from reading simple books to long novels, or that they can suddenly reel off every capital city, speak some German or tell you all about the Roman Empire. Since so much of what is going on is not visible to us, it can feel like things come out of nowhere. In the beginning, you may find yourself comparing your child with children who go to school, and assessing where they might be 'ahead' and where they might be 'behind' compared to their peers. After a while, you'll realize that this is like comparing apples and pears. Where your child finds something interesting and meaningful, they are likely to acquire knowledge at an astonishing rate. But it won't be the same across the board. At different times, I've had a child whose spelling was as good as any adult's and could name every country in the world, but whose writing looked like a spider's. Or a child who hadn't mastered punctuation in English but could read the Russian alphabet and some basic Mandarin and hold their end in any discussion of geopolitics. Where were they compared to their peers? It's impossible to say. Out of school, many parents are amazed, as I was, to see how their children take charge of their own reading and how this looks nothing like the linear progress expected at school.

> I kept reading things about how children do teach themselves to read. My friends' children were reading much earlier and she was almost six and not reading, though we had lots of books and we'd always read to her. I had those moments of, am I doing enough?, but she didn't like any sort of push. She wanted to do things on her terms. And then one day she just picked up a book and started reading." LIANNE

> One of my biggest fears was letting go of teaching the boys how to read, and I was especially concerned about my youngest who flat refused to read anything after he was pushed too hard to read at school. We always read to them at night, and to my complete surprise Teddy announced one night that he wanted to read to me instead. Despite being almost 10 pm, he picked up five early reader books from the back of the book basket and began to read. I casually stocked the basket with new books and he carried on wanting to read to us at night for about six weeks. He has since stopped but I'm okay with this as I can see he's progressing and learning at a pace that's comfortable for him." ANNIE

There is likely to be a lot of delving in and out of different interests

It may feel frustrating that just when your child has embraced a new hobby (and you've bought the book, course, kit, etc.), they are ready to move on to something new. As they explore what is appealing to them, there are likely to be many activities and interests that they delve in and out of. They may focus on one thing for several weeks, only to move on and never look at it again. Perhaps they thought it would be more interesting or enjoyable than it turned out to be. Or maybe they already got what they needed from it or it fed a new idea. This can all feel slippery to hold but your child is exploring and gathering what they need from each thing they delve into. That may, of course, mean establishing some guidelines around how much money can be spent on fledgling activities. Trial classes and borrowed or second-hand kits are definitely a wise way to go.

> Interests don't last for the duration of a school term. They can come and go at the speed of light!" ANNIE

There is unlikely to be any measurable output, so there may be no goal except to satisfy curiosity

None of us can be privy to what is happening in someone else's mind. School tries to get around that by requiring output and using tests to double-check that what is meant to be retained actually is retained. We think we know when a child has learned because there is something for the adult to see. A piece of writing, a poem, a test, a neatly filled-in exercise book. But natural learning, when done freely and without coercion, doesn't offer any of this reassurance. At home, your child may or may not choose to produce things. If they do create some kind of output, this is likely to be for their satisfaction and not for yours. If you come from a long line of people-pleasers, this might be challenging, but perhaps you can also celebrate the fact that your child is learning for their own satisfaction and not for any approval it could bring. And, if you find that the lack of tangible output makes you particularly anxious, take a deep breath and remind yourself that just because you can't see it doesn't mean it isn't happening. Later on in this chapter, you'll find lots of ways to observe how your child is learning that don't involve output.

> The lack of output was difficult for me and it still is! I see that the way I used to see my daughter was a bit two-dimensional. I remember

feeling proud of her good schoolwork and feeling like it meant I was doing okay as a parent, like there was tangible proof that she was okay through her school books or reports. She's fanatical about animals. She doesn't write things down or fill worksheets in, but if you ask her about snakes she could give you GCSE-level knowledge. Now I see that she doesn't need to write things down to know the information. That has really helped me to relax and calm down." RHONDA

I've lost count of the times that an adult has suggested to one of our children that they take an exam in something that they love so that they have something to work for, as though the satisfaction of learning was not a reward in itself. And I am happy to admit that I've made that suggestion myself too. There is a sense in the adult world that if no successful goal is achieved, the learning isn't really valid. Why bother if you can't prove it? But the goal to satisfy curiosity is huge and will almost certainly feel far more important to your child than passing an exam. A couple of years ago someone asked my son why he didn't take an exam in Mandarin so that he had something to aim for. He looked a bit confused, then answered that his aim was to travel to China and to be able to talk to people in Mandarin. His goal was far bigger, but stress-free and extremely motivating to him. Which isn't to say that at some point he won't choose to take an exam, but at that time his own curiosity was plenty enough.

It is near impossible to pull apart the strands of learning into history, geography, chemistry or any other school subject

At some point early on in our journey, I stopped worrying about how things fit into a list of school subjects because it was impossible to pick it all apart. Any attempt I might make at introducing a specific subject generally felt forced and limiting, and far less interesting than the way my children were naturally learning. By observing them, I quickly realized that the neat classification of life into distinct subjects is a school invention and not necessary for a child to learn. After all, real life is not neatly divided into subjects. History, geography, science, languages – everything that ever happens or is thought about involves multiple, interconnected subjects and disciplines. I have come to see my children's minds as ever-expanding 3D models. New information just slots in where it best fits and it just doesn't really matter what the subject is. Having said that, as they get older, our children will almost certainly want to hone in on more specific subjects that they are drawn to, and we can allow ourselves to be guided by them.

> "I was massively challenged. I started by looking at everything through a curriculum lens. So I would be asking myself, what are we ticking in this activity?, whether it was baking a cake, making mud pies in the garden, creating a bug hotel, or reading stories. It took me ages to stop doing that." HOLLY

There is no particular pace to it

Children, just like adults, have rhythms to their lives. There may be days when nothing in particular seems to happen, and other days that are a whirlwind of activity. This is probably one of the hardest aspects of self-directed learning for the parent. The quiet days can easily trigger worry and a panicky questioning of whether this is all enough. But this is an essential part of children becoming familiar with their own rhythms, and learning when they need to regroup, think, relax or unwind. Just like the rest of us. At some point, the quiet times end and something else arises. Here, the conversations or activities that come in busier moments are often connected to something learned or absorbed in that ebb and flow, inspired by a TV programme or a game, or just some random thoughts that had the space to arise.

> "I've noticed that things go in waves, and now I understand that things can go quiet but it doesn't mean they're not interested any more. I started to see that learning isn't this linear process, it's actually all over the place and really messy. Sometimes they might just need one piece of information to move them forward. If they ask something about space, it doesn't mean they want to read a whole book or know everything about space. They just need that curious question

answered for now. Then, when they need more, they will seek out the next piece of information. They know what they need." CLAIRE

Learning is a constant – it doesn't only happen during school hours

When we first started, I would find myself surprised when our children would suddenly be bursting with energy on a Sunday evening with some project. I would find it equally challenging when they were still in pyjamas late on a Monday morning. Aware that everyone else we knew was heading off to work or to school, I felt like we were somehow bunking off. But school hours are a social construct and learning really does happen all the time. Our children's brains don't take the weekends and evenings off.

Of course, that doesn't mean that you have to be on duty 24/7 or eager to engage at all times. Your child may now be much freer, but whether you are working or not, you'll probably still have external obligations that require your time and focus. You'll find that it takes a little while for you all to find your rhythm, and in the beginning it may be disconcerting not to have the stability of school and those fixed learning hours. But remember that unschooling isn't about saying yes to everything all the time or feeling guilty because you can't. It's about working together to make sure everyone is being valued and respected. You'll almost certainly need to think about your own needs and boundaries, and how to discuss these with your child. In Chapter 11 you'll find some ideas about how to best approach that.

> All sorts of things come up. Sometimes we'll be going to bed, and they'll ask a question, and suddenly we'll be learning something about a planet or some kind of mathematical concept because a question's just been asked." JAYNE

> As young adults now, my children both understand that learning is a very personal experience, that it happens in every moment and that they can approach it any way they choose." NICOLA

Children make no distinction between learning and playing

It's easy to fall into the idea that a child who is playing isn't learning. But it's important to remember that not only do children learn through play, but also that your child is unlikely to judge their activities in the same way you do. Adults may assume that academic topics are serious and play is fun, but your child isn't making that distinction (unless they have internalized it from adults). I've seen children move seamlessly between Minecraft and history quizzes and back again, I've spent hours making up sums for a child who loves maths, and watched interests born in video games become intellectual pursuits. What is learning and what is playing? If you can enter their mindset, you will see that there is no difference.

> Charlie is really into Dungeons & Dragons. If he is the Dungeon Master, he tells the story, and takes the other players on a journey, so he has to be very flexible and cooperative with the other players. There's so much in it – leadership skills, problem solving, organizing, planning, interpersonal skills. I think these are hugely important skills that most of us only learn as adults, so I think it's a gift to learn as children. Max has set up a wooden train track, the kind that you wouldn't normally find after the age of five. But he's 13. He was explaining some law of physics and why the train needs to go in a straight line and curvature, and all this engineering stuff. He's exploring all of this through his train set and engineering magazines. He might learn about the laws of physics at school, but it wouldn't be as deep as this, because he's genuinely interested and not trying to please a teacher. Here, there's playfulness and deep learning." EVA

> Just when I was starting to feel triggered by the three hours he'd spent rooted to the spot on his iPad, he called me over to show me what he'd been working on. He'd discovered how to make chemical compounds with access to the elements of the entire periodic table in Minecraft. I had no idea that this even existed in Minecraft. He was

buzzing about it and had no idea he'd taken a deep dive into the world of chemistry." ANNIE

❝ Looking for the wrong evidence can sabotage it all. Or thinking that one thing is more important than another. I played a board game with my son and it turns out that he knows all his times tables. I've never taught him and he didn't set out to learn them. He just plays a lot with numbers and games." HOLLY

Learning will not feel difficult if it's meaningful

Unfortunately, I left school with a fixed idea of what was difficult and what I was bad at. It has taken my children's open-minded approach to life to make me realize that a lot of things I had dismissed (such as chemistry) as incomprehensible to me can actually be interesting and are within my grasp. Unless we make things seem like hard work, there's no reason that our children will assume they are. Science, reading, equations, writing – when these feel interesting or meaningful to a child, they won't be a struggle.

❝ My daughter thinks that she might retain more knowledge because she's more passionate about the things that she's learning. For example, when she's writing a story, she gets to choose if she wants to learn about grammar and punctuation. And it makes sense for her to do that, because it feels purposeful and useful." HAYLEY

They will choose ways to learn and explore that you might not have thought of

When a child is curious about something and in charge of how they explore that particular interest, they will probably find resources that might never occur to us. Some children might enjoy worksheets or school-style books, but if your child avoids these like the plague, they may just be recognizing that these are just not the best tools for the job. From YouTube videos to apps, conversation, books and courses, they are likely to find ways to learn that are far more aligned with how they best acquire information. When a resource no longer works for them, they can move on to something else that serves them better. If you are looking for resources to support your child, be guided by what they naturally choose to engage with.

The real world is an endless source of inspiration

'But how will they deal with the real world?', people might ask you. You'll know when your mindset has started to shift because you'll recognize that this is an odd question. Not only are your children very much part of the real world, but they are likely to be endlessly inspired by it. Whether it's creating their own business, politics, theatre, blacksmithing or nature, they will seek out the experiences and knowledge that help them understand the world better and to acquire the skills they are drawn to. When we think back to the science of learning in Chapter 1 and how children are naturally wired to learn through direct and meaningful experience, it's easy to understand why real life is far more compelling than a classroom.

> " She's really interested in events and organizing, and she recently organized a fundraiser for some rescue goats. She did it all herself and raised over £3000 in an evening. So she's thinking now about taking GCSEs to go to college to study that. She's at a stage now where she wants to work out where she's going and wants to channel her energy into that." LIANNE

They will challenge themselves

Many people assume that a child who has no external obligation to continue with something challenging would give up at the first hurdle. But the power of intrinsic motivation is inspiring to watch in action. Sure, there will be lots of frustration along the way. They may take a break when they're fed up, and sometimes they will know that giving up is the best option, but often, they will rise to incredible challenges they set themselves. In fact, the lack of external pressure means that they are more ready to step up as there is no risk of shame or embarrassment. If they give up, they won't be letting anyone down or feeling the weight of someone else's disappointment, making it much safer to try difficult things.

> She's a very experiential learner, so she has to try things herself. Any idea she has, she doesn't see a barrier to whether it's achievable. Sometimes those ideas have to be reined in a bit because they're not always manageable. But her tenacity to just try something and make mistakes, because no one showed her how to do it, is impressive. She doesn't want to learn in a direct way where someone tells her something; she wants to figure it out for herself. She learns so much in that process about learning and about dealing with disappointment when it goes wrong. She's gotten much better with disappointment. Losing a board game or a drawing not turning out as expected used to cause huge meltdowns. Now, if a project goes wrong, she might be upset, but she takes a break, tidies up, and moves on." DONNA

You might not have a clue how they are learning

We're so used to learning being such an obvious task that the idea that you could be with your children all day and not know what or how they're learning may seem strange. I was baffled at first by all the things they shared with me, as I really couldn't figure out how or when they had come across these things. Sometimes I'd ask them, 'How do you know that?' and often they couldn't pinpoint how they did.

> So they would come up to me and I'd be like, 'Wow, you've learned that skill and I didn't show you.' At one point, that had happened enough times that I could see that I didn't need to see everything. Just because I don't see something doesn't mean it hasn't happened. It's impossible to measure or to know what's going on." HOLLY

> Sometimes I don't know how they know things. They'll say, 'Oh, from telly or something.' Or 'Oh, a friend told us that.' My son will come out with words. And I'm like, 'You know, that's quite advanced vocab. How do you know that?' And he'll say, 'Oh, from a book.'" JAYNE

> "There's that thing where you just want the next step to happen. I really wanted her to swim, so I kept taking her to the pool. One day she did two strokes and I went away really excited and thinking that the next week, then, she'd do three, four, five and so on. But she didn't do it again for three months after that. I realized that she was just playing so didn't necessarily feel like going back to it yet. Then we went away for a month, and although she was in the pool lots and always really enjoyed it, she didn't swim a stroke. When we came back, we went to the pool with our home ed friends. I saw her lined up at the deep end with all friends all about to jump in, and I was thinking stop, you can't swim!, but she jumped in and swam the whole length. So all that playing and understanding the water, all of that had been quietly going on." LIANNE

They'll seek out teachers when they need them

None of this means that our children won't also seek out teachers. They are likely to look for and find teachers, mentors and role models who help them learn and explore the things that interest them. They may want to join online or in-person courses around a specific topic. Or there could be a friend or neighbour who is knowledgeable in an area that fascinates them. When your child is able to engage freely and willingly and in a format that feels right for them, learning with a teacher or mentor is likely to be far more satisfying and inspiring than it would be in a big classroom in which there are almost certainly a number of children who would prefer not to be there at all.

How will you know your child is learning?

It's a big piece of work to trust the process, but your child is always learning. Although you probably won't get any school-style output as proof, and you won't be ticking off any learning boxes, there will be many clues throughout the day about everything they are learning and the paths they are following, each of which I will discuss in more detail:

- Questions
- Conversations
- New skills
- Plans and ideas
- Their mood.

Questions

You'll get clues about what your child is curious about through the questions they ask. But beware of making assumptions. A question about the pyramids or a remote island in the Pacific may raise your hopes of a deep dive into Ancient Egypt or world geography, and that may well be the case. But equally, the question may be just a small stepping stone on the way to somewhere else. Some children may ask lots of questions and some may not. They may appreciate a long, detailed answer, but probably not. So, enjoy watching your child's natural curiosity in action and be interested in the questions, but try to not grab hold of them! (More about that in Chapter 8.)

Conversations

You'll know your child is learning by the conversations they want to have. If they have been pondering some subject or feeling enthusiastic or curious about an interest, they may well want to mull it over with someone else, perhaps to clarify something, or to just share their enthusiasm. Or maybe they are grappling with some aspect of life or the wider world and need some help to figure it all out. If we pay attention to these conversations, we will see a huge amount of curiosity, learning and joining of dots. A lot of home-educating families find that casual conversations are one of the main sources of learning and connection in their home. These conversations are far more interesting and joyful when we are not looking for the learning but simply enjoying the conversation. A relaxed sharing of thoughts is invitational and fun for everyone. Quizzing our children on their knowledge, not so much.

> " I think one of the biggest realizations is that lots of my children's

learning comes from our conversations. Teddy has been really interested in the Ukraine conflict since getting to know a Ukrainian boy locally. Perhaps it's a bit heavy for a six-year-old but he is so curious about what is happening and why. His questions have ranged from why Russia is at war with Ukraine, to which countries are on Ukraine's side, to what an ally is. I've helped him find the answers to these questions and, despite nothing being written down, he remembers so much of it. For me, this has been such a powerful lesson – the value of learning and retaining information through conversation alone. This is also true with maths. He hates any kind of workbook but will happily lie in bed at night and ask you to throw out sums for him to solve." ANNIE

" A lot of our learning is verbal and I've realized that my children are just this way inclined and so am I. So that's a shift I've had to make – to not needing evidence. They can listen to things and have conversations, and they will learn from that. So I make time for that. You just have to listen and you just have to be available." JAYNE

New skills
A foreign language, a craft, a new game, a dance... What skills is your child engaging with? It's important we don't get stuck on our own perceived value of the skill itself. Observe instead everything it requires of your child, such as dedication, the ability to persevere, to rise to a challenge, follow complex instructions, use their initiative or step outside of their comfort zone. These are skills that they will apply to other things too.

Plans and ideas
We can often get a sense of the threads our children are following by the future things they are drawn to. Maybe they're talking about travel, starting a business or some new project they'd like to do. These 'real world' plans can be filled with incredible learning journeys, and it can be hard not to jump on them and want to help our children make them into a reality. Conversely, we may be tempted to dismiss them as wild

flights of fantasy. But if we can listen and really pay attention, we'll understand more about the motivation behind these ideas and which aspects of them are particularly appealing to our child. Then we can see if there's a part of it that we can support them with.

Their mood

Are they lit up by something? Are they bursting with enthusiasm, or so focused you could hear a pin drop? You can tell when something feels meaningful to your child. And if it feels meaningful to them, you can guarantee that they're learning.

If you don't pay attention, you might miss it

While we are still in a fixed mindset, and looking for the kind of learning we might see at school, we are likely to miss much of what I have discussed here. We will be focused on looking for what we expect to see and worrying about all the things that aren't happening. So, instead of a child resting and gathering resources for something new, we see a child not doing anything. Instead of a child making an informed choice, we see a child who can't stick at things. Instead of a child excelling and rising to a challenge, we see a child wasting time on a game. We cut conversations short because we think they need to be getting on with things. Or we bore our children with long answers to short questions and put them off asking us again. Ironically, we can easily kill the learning that is happening by worrying that no learning is happening.

> " You don't always see the learning in the moment. It's difficult because you want everything to be really tangible and obvious, but it's not. And sometimes you're not going to see that piece until years in the future, and that's hard. But when they were at school I heard nothing about their day. Now, G talks to me all the time. He's chosen to do some online lessons, and after the lessons he'll often come to find me to tell me what he's done and everything about it. He then teaches

me what he's learned. He is constantly learning, exploring and sharing his knowledge." CLAIRE

Write it all down

In the early days, when things still feel a little unsure, it can be helpful to write down all the things that do happen. As you look over the days and weeks, you'll notice how much is really taking place and you'll spot certain threads and recurring themes. You could try noting down the following: interesting conversations, questions, things that lit them up, challenges they took on, new interests, plans and ideas, resources they're using, games they're playing. Use this journal to reassure yourself in wobbly moments.

> At the beginning, I kept a diary app and I could just post pictures there. It was a really helpful way to do it. I actually did write a few assessment and planning kind of entries to help with my own thinking about where everybody was at, and identifying places where I thought there might need some work to be done. So that was really helpful scaffolding for me, because I was creating my own evidence that I could then look back on without putting pressure on the children to do things. It's your evidence, but you're not forcing them to kind of write beautiful reams of things and produce notebooks and all that kind of stuff." JAYNE

The power of allowing your child the space to explore and connect

When a child is struggling in a school environment, the perspective is often entirely outcome-focused and on trying to fix the things that seem broken. The external pressure and worry leave little space for the child to explore or to connect with their own compass.

Donna talks about how that negative perspective impacted her and her daughter, and describes beautifully how transformational it was for her to let go of outcomes and to pay attention instead to the present moment. As she moved away from the idea that learning had to look a certain way, and started to trust her daughter, she realized how much lighter life was and how much richness was right there in their everyday lives together:

> When you're in school and it's really difficult, and your child's got additional needs and learning differences, there's a heavy language that gets used around it all, like deficit, comorbidity, disorder… And then all this support piles in, and experts who are analysing this and that, and everyone's under scrutiny. Your child's under scrutiny. You're under scrutiny. The school feels under scrutiny. Everyone's defensive and everyone's hackles are up. It is easy to be in a pit of despair because that headspace is so negative. It seems like the focus is on all the things that are going wrong, then more and more seems to go wrong, and every step feels like another failure. That's where we were, in this negative spiral. But if you just turn things on their head and drop expectations, you can see what's actually there. And there's loads there. There is just so much that is spontaneously happening. And then you look for connections, and as you keep connecting and showing an interest in things, new things emerge and come to the surface. Perhaps these things were there all along, but you weren't paying attention to them before. Then all these little seeds start to germinate, like wild flowers on a lawn that's been mown for 20 years. Even seeds that I might have sown a long time ago that I thought were buried. When you stop mowing the lawn, the flowers come back and suddenly the wild returns. And it's abundant and joyful. The butterflies come, the bees come, and then new birds come, and it just does its own thing. It feels like that is what's happening in our lives."

Journal prompts

- Which aspects of self-directed learning do you find the most challenging?

- And which do you most enjoy?

- How do you know what your child is learning about? Do they share with you? Do they like to talk about things? Are you making time and space for conversation?

Chapter summary

- Unlike traditional schooling, the focus of self-directed learning is on the journey rather than specific outcomes. Children explore their interests deeply, developing lifelong learning habits through curiosity and independent decision-making.

- Self-directed learning is non-linear and unpredictable. Children might deep dive into all sorts of unexpected things, while other interests will come and go. It can look quite confusing from the outside!

- Children are driven by curiosity and personal interests. Without external pressures, they set and manage their own challenges.

- In the absence of tests or assignments you'll know your child is learning by paying attention to your day-to-day interactions and conversations with them.

- Real life provides endless meaningful learning opportunities and, like real life, learning is happening all the time. It isn't confined to subjects or timetables.

Chapter 4

Holding the space for your child

You've probably realized that if we want our children to live fully into who they are, to learn at their own pace, and to be able to set and advocate for their boundaries, then mainstream parenting advice isn't going to be of much use to us. Most parenting approaches are based on the assumption that the parent always knows best, and emphasize control and authority, with the sole purpose of getting children to comply. This dynamic is deeply ingrained in our society, where it's considered normal for adults to exercise power and coercion over children to make sure things go their way. Sometimes this may look quite benign, but we might ask ourselves in what other relationships would such a power dynamic be acceptable. In fact, if I am ever unsure about whether I've spoken to one of my children from a place of power, I ask myself if what I said would have sounded acceptable in the context of an adult relationship or friendship. If the answer is no, then I've fallen into old habits and overstepped the mark.

Unschooling isn't so much about shifting the power as it is about moving away from the concept of power and coercion altogether. It embraces an entirely different paradigm, one which understands that the parent isn't here to mould or control, but to be their child's ally. Rather than directing them, our role is to hold a safe space within which they can grow, learn and explore. This means deschooling ourselves of many notions about parenting that we are likely to have acquired along the way. In this chapter we're going to look at what it means to hold space, and why this way of living with our children may initially be deeply challenging but is ultimately far more fulfilling and joyful for us all.

Accompanying our children on a journey

We could imagine this idea of holding space as accompanying our children on a journey they are taking. If we don't trust them to make good choices, or simply believe that it's the parent's job to always be in charge, we would choose the destination ourselves. Perhaps we'd choose it because we consider it to be the safest destination or because it's the one that most guarantees success in the world. To get there, we might make our child take the route that we once took ourselves because it feels familiar and worked well enough for us. Or we might insist that they take an entirely different route because we got it so wrong. In either case, we would map out the path and walk ahead of our child, showing them which roads to take, and correcting them if they are tempted by some attractive detour that isn't in the plan. We may hurry them along to get them to our chosen destination as soon as possible, getting annoyed or promising a reward at the end if they keep our pace. Or we just could fill their heads with all our notions about failure or success, ensuring they internalize our voice so effectively that we no longer need to worry about them straying off the path.

If, instead, we were to assume that to not be coercive or controlling we just had to leave our child to it, the journey would look very different. Our child might go on ahead as we trailed some way behind. Not wanting to get in their way, we might be so far back that they can't check in with us when they're not sure which road to take, or ask for a helping hand or a comforting hug when they take a wrong turn. We wouldn't be able to share thoughts on potential pitfalls or dangers that we might know something about, offer companionship on a long, boring stretch, or just share the joy of beautiful landscapes. We might lose sight of them completely, or maybe they would feel so overwhelmed at being alone that they make little progress.

When we hold space for our children, we don't know what the destination will be. However, we do know that by giving them the space and support they need, they will grow in their capacity to know what the best next step looks like. They may choose paths that we would never have gone down and that hold no appeal for us. In this case, we can be curious and open to learning more about their choices. They might sometimes want us right next to them, and other times prefer to stride ahead, pushing beyond us and their own comfort zone. They may wander down some enticing path and then decide it's not for them after all and turn back again. In all this, we're close by if they need us, neither directing them nor leaving them to it. If we have some useful information, we can share it with them. We might help out by taking on some aspect of the journey that feels too much for them, such as researching possibilities or offering to go ahead to check it's all safe. If something feels uncomfortable to us, we might need to talk things through with them. Sometimes it will feel good to just walk along together for a while and enjoy each other's company. Above all, there is no rush to get to the destination, because we both understand that the journey itself is just as valuable.

> It very much feels like I'm alongside them, like we're on this kind of path together. And it's going to be great sometimes and it's going to be not so great sometimes. But we're in it together and we've got their backs. So when something is going really well, or something wonderful happens, we celebrate it. When there's something that's tricky, I'm with them in it and I will help them however I can." JAYNE

> I've got an image of me walking alongside my children rather than ahead or behind them. I see myself as a joint discoverer, and I suppose I will do less of that as they get older and they will want to discover things more and more on their own. I see my role as creating a safe space where they feel free to explore themselves without feeling judged or that there are expectations." EVA

❝ My role is to make my children feel supported in how they like to spend their time, and to provide a safe and nurturing space where they feel relaxed and able to explore their interests. I think the most important part is to be available to them when they need me, to be on hand when they need help researching something or to chat through their thoughts and ideas." ANNIE

❝ I guess I feel like my role is just to hold space. A space for her to explore and to feel safe and held, because she struggles to feel safe in the world. Then from that place, she can manoeuvre, be creative and curious, and try things. Then she can come back to not wanting to try things for a bit. It's definitely not about teaching and imparting knowledge, which is what I was afraid of in the beginning." DONNA

It's hard to let go of what we think it should all look like

No matter how logical and appealing this notion of holding space feels, it's surprisingly difficult to be with our children and resist the urge to direct them. Most of us have a clear picture in our heads of what a good childhood should look like. Sleep, learning, food, technology, nature, reading, helping around the house, cooking, creating, engaging with others – think about any of these for just a few minutes and you'll probably notice that you have a strong sense of how you would like that to look for your child. It might look similar to your childhood, or it might purposefully look quite different. Many of us take the best bits of our own childhoods, add in all the things we would have also liked, and then pile on top everyone else's expectations of us and our children. Not only do we set the bar outrageously high, but since our child is not the child we once were, our particular version of what is right may be significantly different from theirs. You may also realize that you have assumptions about your child's future, such as that they will go to university or have a certain career path – in which case, it will be hard for you not to be overly attached to choices they make and not feel some dread when their choices don't align with that future.

Even though our desire may be to make our children's lives as wonderful as possible (or at least to not get it all wrong), the more we impose our version of an ideal life onto them, the less space we give them to live into being themselves and creating a life that feels meaningful to them. If you catch yourself feeling worried when they don't take a particular path, you might want to spend a little while pondering why this is so important to you. You can ask yourself the following questions:

- Is this tied up with your idea of what a good parent is?
- Do you worry about what other people may say?
- Does it feel like something else would be a failure?
- How would it feel to open up to other possibilities?

Accompanying your child without trying to alter their course may well be one of the hardest things you ever do. I love Annie's analogy of this process as sailing with her two children on an unmanned ship:

> I think at the start of the process we want to have *all* the answers so we don't mess it up. It's a huge change from school life. It takes time and patience to adapt to how your children want to spend their time. It's so tempting to bulldoze in and divert their attention when you're feeling like they could be doing something more useful. I feel like some days I'm sailing an unmanned ship and it can be really uncomfortable. My two children might spend hours doing something that I honestly struggle to see the value in. But then in days and weeks to come, there's always a shift and the unmanned ship ends up on a beautiful island. Somewhere I could have never led them to." ANNIE

What qualities do we bring to the space?

To be able to hold a space in which our child feels confident to learn and explore what it is to be their whole self, there are some qualities that we can start to intentionally cultivate. Don't worry if some of these feel a little out of reach right now – we'll be looking at how to develop them in future chapters.

Trust

Read any book about self-directed learning or listen to any podcast and this is the word that comes up over and over again. Cultivating trust in ourselves, in our children, and in the process itself is essential for us to hold this space confidently. In a trusting space, our child feels relaxed, capable and responsible, more able to take on new challenges, make decisions and ultimately trust themselves. And when we trust our children, we initiate a happy virtuous circle. The more we trust, the more we see, and so the more we trust.

Frustratingly, although trust is probably the most important piece in all this, it is also extremely difficult to possess in the beginning. There are some oft-quoted words by John Holt (the New York educator who first coined the term 'unschooling'): 'To trust children we must first learn to trust ourselves…and most of us were taught as children that we could not be trusted' (2017, p.xiii). Indeed, how can you trust something you've never seen before and were not allowed to experience yourself as a child? How can you set that virtuous circle spinning when you are full of doubt? I know from my own experience that real trust is built on all the numerous little things that happen day in, day out, and that takes time. It takes time to notice all the ways our children are learning and growing and to relax a little in the knowledge that this really does work. For most parents, between deciding to take this route and then living with real trust there is the *leap-of-faith stage*. This may be the stage you're in right now, or about to enter, and it can be a fragile place, filled with panicky moments and tons of self-doubt. As you'll see in later chapters, those fraught moments are an inevitable part of the path to trusting and also your greatest place of learning.

❝ One of the most annoying things about this is that you can't rush it. You can find your community, do your research and all the courses, if that's what you need to do. But you're not going to sink into it until you see it happen, and that can take a long time. A big one for me was my daughter learning to read. It looked like she learned overnight, but I'd been watching her for months and months. She would ask me questions, follow my finger when I read to her, and notice that sometimes words don't make the sounds you'd think they would. Like why doesn't 'ocean' have a 'sh' in it? Gradually, she stopped asking me so much. Then we were having a Chinese takeaway and she just read the fortune cookie. In the beginning, you're trusting blindly, and then, slowly, you get the evidence that it's working so you can relax and trust some more. It's a combination of trust and time, and time will bring the evidence." HOLLY

❝ As I started working on myself, the pressure came off, and I eased off on the kids a bit. This gave them more space. I was learning how to not put out their fire and how to facilitate rather than teach. Everyone believes that children need to be taught, and the more I watch my kids, the more I think that's wrong. They need your support, and sometimes there will be something they don't understand, and you help them. But if it's always that the adult knows everything, and the adult knows best, you can really squish them, and I felt that they were sort of squished. The more I stepped away, the more they came out of themselves and explored their interests. Suddenly there was room for their ideas and they started to step forward and do things themselves." CLAIRE

Curiosity

Curiosity has probably become my favourite word on this journey, and we'll be taking a deep dive into this transformational quality in Chapter 10. For now, suffice to say that curiosity is our best friend whenever we're struggling to trust or understand. It allows us to get beyond surface behaviours, spot nuances and see things in new ways. And, of course, staying open-minded and receptive not only rewards us with interesting new perspectives and information, but it is also a great quality to model to our children. When we feel curious, we are always in a learning and exploratory frame of mind.

> When she came out of school, suddenly there was this huge gap and initially, it felt like a really negative space. We seem to assume that unless we tell them what to do and make them do it they'll fail. So I tried all these learning things and she wouldn't engage with any of it. Finally, I had to stop banging my head against the wall and just notice. And when I started to do that, the space began to change." RHONDA

An empowering lens

Even in the most caring educational environment, there is a powerful tendency to see some children, particularly neurodivergent children, in terms of what they can't do. Although the intention may be to best meet their needs, the focus, unfortunately, becomes centred on all the ways they struggle compared to their peers, the things they need to work on, and all the ways in which life and learning must be adapted for them. Within the school system, it can be hard for the parent to not also adopt this lens and to look at their child in terms of the things that are 'wrong' when that's the dominant narrative.

One of the most liberating aspects of not being in a school system is that we can choose to see our children through an entirely different lens. That is not to say that we shouldn't recognize the specific challenges that our children need help with. But, out of school, aspects of your child's way of being that seemed difficult or complicated in a classroom no longer need to be laden with worry. Instead, we can navigate these alongside our children, understanding that just as they have certain challenges, so they also have wonderful gifts. We can help them build up confidence in other areas, so that they can engage with the harder things with more confidence. We can hold our children in a gaze that isn't searching for issues or looking for what needs to be fixed, but that lets them know that they are whole just as they are. In fact, when you create an environment that genuinely meets your child's needs, many of the things that felt problematic at school may well just fade away.

> I realized that a lot of the stress in our lives was coming from external sources, like school. When we took those things away it became a lot more simple. I was able to just really observe who they were. My role is to be their biggest fan, just a massive advocate for them, and a facilitator. Walking alongside but also learning and knowing when to nudge them a little or encourage them and when to hang back. It's like a little dance, but you're always walking alongside and you're listening and being very present with them, being available and being a calm and safe space." CLAIRE

Non-judgement

It's natural to want our children to make choices that serve them well, but we need to be careful not to pretend we're respecting their autonomy only to roll our eyes when their choices are not aligned with ours. For our children to be free to live into their full selves, we have to relinquish the notion that a good parent is always right. If we are derisive about their choices, we risk undermining our relationship and the trust we're building. Would you share your new adventures in self-directed learning with a friend who previously told you that you were making a terrible choice? Probably not. If we want our children to know that we are willing companions on their journey, we need to ensure that the space we hold feels open and safe, and that means avoiding being their judge or critic. There will be lots of things we need to have conversations with our children about, but when we approach as an ally, the exploration of any topic can be far richer. And, if we were to save our approval only for the things we like, we would risk sending our children down the people-pleasing route, where the better option always becomes the one that gains someone else's approval.

> One of the most important things is not to judge. One of my biggest roles, I suppose, was keeping a safe space in terms of them feeling loved and accepted, and that they could talk to us, and that they could make mistakes and always come to us if they thought they'd done something silly." HAYLEY

Connection

As we saw in Chapters 1 and 2, there is nothing more important than your relationship with your child. Knowing that they are loved and valued is the solid ground from which they know they can venture out, explore, make mistakes, get things wrong, and always be held with compassion. Parenting can easily descend into an interminable to-do list, and we can find ourselves so busy running around that we don't invest in our relationships with our children. So find your language of love with your child and connect regularly with them. For a younger child who you spend much time in close contact with, this might be quite easy. For an older child or one who enjoys a high level of autonomy in their interests, think about what little acts can help you connect. Take them a cup of tea or a snack, show genuine interest in what they're doing, or invite them out for something you both enjoy, such as a walk or going to the cinema. Let them be aware of the soft edges of the space you hold for them. Something I have appreciated about our children not being at school is that learning has rarely been a cause for friction. Instead, it has been a source of enjoyment and connection and brought endless opportunities for sharing knowledge and enriching each other.

> Maintaining communication with them is important to me and it helps me feel relaxed. So, just touching in with them every day with physical connection and verbal connection, and letting them tell me if they need anything." NICOLA

Safety

All these qualities combine to create a safe space for your child. This is essential for all children, but if your child has been anxious or has recently had a difficult time at school and is in a phase of burnout, then the safety that your presence offers will be even more needed. This may sometimes feel overwhelming for you, and your ability to regulate your own nervous system will help you both enormously – we will work more on this in Part 2. Holding space for an anxious or dysregulated child requires an enormous amount of strength and emotional energy, so don't underestimate your own needs.

> " When I changed my mindset, she started to tell me more about what she was doing because she could trust me. She was so relieved. She was in a mental crisis at the time, having panic attacks every day and not leaving the house. I think that if she hadn't had such a big breakdown she might still be attending school by the skin of her teeth, but I feel she is much better off now because of what has happened. She's learned how to regulate emotionally and learned so much about herself and I've had to learn to trust her. I had consistent things like walks in the countryside with the dog. I love sewing and dressmaking and tried to do some of that every day, even when I was really struggling with it all. That was really calming." RHONDA

Joy

I was talking with a parent recently whose child had just left school, and they described how they felt a constant sense of 'impending doom'. The responsibility they felt to make this work for their child was adding a huge weight to the days and making it seem like every single little detail really mattered. It's easy to understand why they would feel like this, and it's also easy to see how their child is likely to pick up on the weightiness of their parent's feelings and all the inherent expectations. This can quickly set off a downward spiral and end up with a tense home in which no one can thrive. We can't be bright and breezy 24/7, and nor would we probably want to be. However, we can look after ourselves as best we can and work out what we need in order to hold things a little more lightly. It's inevitable that when our own cup is filled, things feel easier and less worrisome. We take the ups and downs less personally, we have more energy and more patience, and we are less likely to be triggered into fearful patterns. Any suggestions we make from this place will also sound far more appealing to our children. And showing that our happiness is important to us is a beautiful invitation to our children to make their happiness important to them too.

None of this means that you have to pretend to feel cheerful when you're feeling down, or that you should ever feel bad about how you are feeling. But, as you deschool and work your way through the worries and fears, you will naturally feel lighter and more joyful about life with your child. And when you don't, you'll have the tools on hand to help you.

It may feel neglectful at first

At first, allowing our children more autonomy and choice can feel extremely uncomfortable. You might even feel like you are being neglectful if you're not trying to constantly cajole them into being busy or into doing things that appear more educational. You'll almost certainly wonder what other people would think, and probably conclude that they would think you were doing nothing. You might well think about how busy your child would be all day if they were at school, and feel like you should be recreating something similar. But, facilitating our children's learning from a place of connection is entirely different from pushing or directing it. And, as you let go of the idea that you must be leading them and settle into this as a journey of discovery, you'll find yourself embracing something far more nuanced and satisfying.

> Other people might look in and think the parent isn't really doing anything. I sometimes wonder if it looks neglectful. I think that in the early days, I needed to prove that it could all work so I ended up dominating the space. But the sign of a good facilitator is that they look like they're doing nothing. They don't need to prove anything, dominate the space or make it about themselves and their own needs." CLAIRE

> At the beginning, I was constantly thinking about learning in absolutely everything we did. I had an ongoing dialogue looking for approval from myself. So I was breaking things up into subjects and saying

it's okay to do this because they're learning that. I would make these diagrams and brainstorm a project for the term, then go to an art gallery, for example, as it tied into the project. It was reassuring, and that approach was helpful for me as I was able to be focused and creative without getting overwhelmed by the thought that we could be doing absolutely anything today. I had some guilt recently because I haven't done that for a while. But that's been an interesting process because while I perceived it as a bit neglectful, Charlie's confidence has exploded. So it's been a huge lesson for me, that as I started giving him more space, and not having my agenda or my expectations on him, his confidence grew." EVA

It's an ever-evolving space

You'll notice how holding space constantly shifts and changes, expanding and contracting according to your child's needs. For a child who feels confident and eager to exert their independence and explore, you may hold the space more loosely, touching in lightly to let them know that you're there. Another child, or that same child on another day, may have a strong need to feel safe and reassured and want their space held more tightly. And as your child grows older, you will certainly find the space changing in new and possibly challenging ways. Where once it felt quite constant from one day to the next, now there might be whole days or weeks of expansion, followed by periods of far closer holding.

Just like their learning, their emotional growth isn't linear, and every child will mature and find independence in their own time and way. You may find that your eight-year-old requires you to hold the space more loosely than your 14-year-old. Or that after a surge of independence and expansion into the world, your teenager seems to need more guidance and closeness. Forget about how you thought it would look, or how anyone else thinks it should look, and just keep returning to your relationship with your child, their needs and what feels right to you both.

Being with your child all day

Many parents find the thought of being with their child all day quite overwhelming. It certainly can be a big shift, particularly if your child is young and you need to be physically present with them for much of the day. And, if you are used to the pressure of coming up with ideas to keep everyone busy at weekends and during the holidays, you are likely to be feeling that same pressure to create busy lives when they're at home all day. Something you will discover quite quickly is that life feels very different when you're in each other's company a lot. You're likely to find a rhythm together, which includes busy moments, together moments, and times you each get on with your own thing.

> It feels horrible to say it but the fears were around just not being able to cope with being with my child all day long. The levels of distress were so high I felt like I needed a break to recalibrate myself and to be able to handle it. I looked forward to when she was at school so I could go for a run, cry, tidy the house, or just do the shopping. We were in survival mode and I needed that time because my nervous system was a mess, my headspace wasn't good, and I saw everything negatively. When I took her out of school, I found that being at home and spending time together was a happy relief. We got along fine, her nervous system had time to recalibrate, and so did mine. Once I relaxed and observed, I saw how different we were, and how different our home life was. We started to regulate for longer periods, coming out of survival mode, and becoming more present and interested." DONNA

> I would get six hours a day when they were at school, but the build-up before and the meltdowns afterwards (particularly my PDA daughter) would be so extraordinary, plus the recovery at the weekends. It would be so distressing for our nervous systems that actually having them at home is much easier for keeping an even keel because if they've had a bad night's sleep or they're coming down with a cold or just having a bad day, we can adjust and do something else. There isn't that manic rushing which means you have to overlook the signs of what people

need and what rest they need. I think people worry about how intense it will be with their kids to be with them 24/7 because they're imagining what it's like in the holidays. But when it's your day-to-day, it's not so intense. Everybody gets into their own rhythms; you're not in each other's pockets all the time. Once you've eased into it, it's not like holiday mode at all. It's far more relaxed than that." HOLLY

❝ What we learned in those first years was how to be together as a family unit, which is something we'd never really done before. Home education changed the dynamic of my relationship with my children. It becomes more balanced, so it doesn't feel so much like parent and children. There's none of that 'Have you got dressed?' 'Where's your bag?' 'Let's go!' It becomes about what we each bring to this unit, and everyone brings something." NICOLA

❝ The reality of all being together in the same space all day long was initially much harder than I thought it would be. But it shifted when I realized I didn't have to be 'on' every minute of the day. When you're on holiday or it's Christmas, it's okay to be 'on' because it's energizing and different. But you can't sustain that. There are going to be days when the kids don't want to do anything, and days when you don't want to do anything. There will be times when you want to get out of the house, and they don't. Managing all that is crucial. Knocking back those expectations was key." JAYNE

Learning to trust

Although there is an inevitable time factor in acquiring trust, you can certainly speed up the process. A big reason why we don't trust in the beginning is because we can't see any evidence to hold on to. Our old narratives around learning and parenting are still very much alive and continually reinforced around us, so we can't quite relax into believing this will really work. As you'll see in future chapters, we are primed to be suspicious of the unknown and to cling to the known.

You can help yourself learn to trust more quickly by making the unknown feel more tangible and familiar. There is a wealth of books and podcasts on alternative ways to learn, filled with other people's research and experiences. Dive into these and start to intentionally build up the new narrative in your mind. When you're having a wobbly moment, put a podcast on and listen to someone who has trodden this path before. Finding people in your local area to connect with in person or joining a supportive online community can also be incredibly helpful for building up confidence while you're still in that rather scary leap-of-faith stage. You'll know when the trust is setting in because things will start to feel far clearer and you'll feel more relaxed. As you support your children to grow in their capacity to navigate life and learning, you'll stop fearing for the future and begin to enjoy watching life unfold.

Hayley and Nicola, who both have adult children, describe this trust:

> " I don't really worry about the future of my children at all because I have absolute faith in them. I feel like whatever life throws at them, they'll deal with it. It's not that they're not going have troubles, and there are things at the moment in our lives that are difficult and challenging, but deep down I know they'll learn from it. And I think I'm very lucky, because I've had that time with my children. I've been able to listen to them, hear what they say and see them in action, so I have been able to build up that bank of trust in them." **HAYLEY**

> " I have total faith in my children. They have a wholeness about them that inspires me – they managed to maintain all of the parts of themselves that were under threat of being diminished. I never worry about their future. They are resilient, adaptable, curious, passionate, kind, communicative and boundaried." **NICOLA**

Journal prompts

- What qualities do you think you bring to the space?
- What qualities would you like to cultivate?
- What would help you cultivate them?

Chapter summary

- Holding space involves creating a safe environment where your child can explore their interests and learn at their own pace. It requires us to be their ally rather than their judge or critic.

- It's extremely hard to let go of our conditioned beliefs of how our children should be and what they should do, and to resist the desire to direct our children to where we want them to go.

- To hold space confidently, we need to cultivate certain qualities such as trust, curiosity, non-judgement and connection. This can take time.

- The space we hold is constantly evolving and shifting with our children's changing needs. We should be flexible and able to hold our children more closely or more loosely depending on how they are and the support they need from us.

- Once we understand how to hold space, focusing more on how we are than what we're doing, being with our children all day becomes far easier.

Chapter 5

But what do I actually do?

It took a while for me to understand the concept of holding space. In the beginning, I assumed my primary role was to fill life with things to keep everyone busy and learning. I had a stack of files packed with leaflets about days out, museums, courses and activities, and I probably spent a couple of hours every evening online researching things we could do and resources they (or I?) would enjoy, from online educational apps to kitchen science projects and crafty ideas. In real life, things rarely panned out how I'd imagined they would, and I'm amazed now at how naively I assumed they would be delighted to follow my lead.

However, although I learned the lesson that this is as much about how we are as what we actually do, there is still plenty of doing involved. The huge difference is that this doing comes from a place of trust and connection and is in partnership with our children. This is markedly different from the relentless, and quite stressful 'It's up to me to lead the way' kind of doing that I initially embarked on. When we think we know best, want to tick a box or need to soothe our own worries, our attempts at doing will almost certainly fall flat and create resistance. But there are still many ways to actively help our children that both support their autonomy and learning, as well as nurture our relationship with them.

There are no fixed rules

There are no set rules about how much we organize or how involved we are in the things our children do. You'll be continually working out when you're needed to help out, nudge something along or take the lead, and when it's best that you hold back and let them work it out. What you do will also depend on numerous factors, such as your child's age, whether they like to spend a lot of time with other children, their interests and how they're feeling that day. If you have more than one child, you'll probably notice that they each require different kinds and levels of support from you – the suggestions and help that are welcomed by one child could feel controlling and directive to another. You may have a child who often wants you to help them figure things out, and you may have a child who prefers to go about things in their own way. And, of course, your child is always growing and evolving, so over time, the ways in which you support them will also naturally shift and change.

As with many aspects of parenting, the best way to know how it's all going is to pay attention to how it feels. When your child wants and appreciates your input, things are likely to flow and feel easy. If your involvement undermines their autonomy or isn't welcome, you'll feel the energy shift as expectations, perceived or real, suck the joy out of the room. As your child naturally defends their space, things are likely to feel more resistant.

Facilitate their interests

One of the most important things you'll do is support your child in their interests. This may be with practical help such as buying supplies, looking for courses and books, or taking them to groups and clubs. Or it may be by joining in, talking things through with them or just lending an interested ear. The younger your child is, the more likely you'll be called upon to be a companion in their interests. If they like similar things to you, this will probably feel quite comfortable, and if not, you may well find yourself far outside your comfort zone, and grappling with things you haven't a clue about. One of the joys (and challenges) of this way of living and learning is how much everyone in the family learns from each other. You're likely to find yourself immersed in activities you'd never given a second thought to, from competing on Duolingo or creating electronic circuits, to drawing anime or looking for frogs in local ponds. And if your child loves technology and you don't, you may need to brace yourself for a sharp learning curve as you wrestle with game design programs and figure out Minecraft mods. Sometimes this will be a lot of fun, and sometimes it may feel boring and difficult. You'll find more in later chapters about taking care of yourself and about how to understand and advocate for your own boundaries when things feel a bit much.

Besides helping your child as they figure out what they need, you can also be keeping an eye out for other things that might fit with their interests or expand on them in some way. Although my children are older now and mostly find what they need themselves, I still take note of anything that I think might be of interest, whether that's a film, a local event or a new club. Keeping an eye on local notice boards and home ed Facebook groups can also turn up unexpected gems. And I've often found that casual conversations with friends, neighbours and friends of friends have opened the door to ideas, activities or inspiring people.

> " I do my best to expand on their areas of interest and offer suggestions of hands-on activities we could do. For example, my youngest son really enjoyed David Walliams' book *Grandpa's Great Escape*, which featured the Imperial War Museum and a thrilling break-in so Grandpa could take his last flight in a Spitfire. So we took a trip to the museum to see the Spitfire and spent the day looking at the museum's other exhibits. My eldest is really in to YouTube videos of science experiments so we replicate what we can at home. Recently, I ordered a bucket of alginate so he and his brother could cast their hands in plaster of Paris. This process was so much fun, although we now have some incredibly realistic, if not slightly creepy, set of cast hands that we have to look at every day!" ANNIE

Bring the world in

I've appreciated over the years how there is nothing more interesting and inspiring to children than real life. We talked in Chapter 1 about how and why human beings are primed to learn what is meaningful to them, so of course children are fascinated by the world around them. Not only do they need to figure out how to thrive in the world right now, but they are also aware that at some point they'll be out there making their living and creating a life that works for them. We can help them be aware of all the possibilities the world holds, and encourage them to feel into the things that are interesting and meaningful to them from a young age.

I remember someone once telling me that one of the reasons they felt school was so important was that otherwise their children wouldn't be exposed to such a big variety of skills and topics. I think that with just a little effort, you can do exactly this out of school. Something I have found fascinating has been how each of my children has deep interests that I neither share nor introduced them to. Without any intentional input from an adult, they must have come across something – maybe through a conversation, a book, a game or a friend – and decided to follow that thread just because it felt right to them. It doesn't take much to plant a seed, and certainly not a whole term of lessons. Other things I did try to intentionally introduce because I thought they were necessary or enriching never took root and were quickly forgotten.

So bring it all in, without expectations, from work, finances and dream jobs to current affairs, hobbies, arts and travel plans. Whether you're talking about the news, a real-life dilemma that you're grappling with, or projects you'd like to do in the future, invite your children into real life as much as you can. There are endless ways to keep the environment rich – share your hobbies with them, invite interesting friends around, discuss politics, find some good documentaries, volunteer or go out into the community and meet interesting people.

❝ Your role definitely changes as they get older. When they're younger, there is a lot more of facilitating their learning, because they don't know what's out there. So there's a lot of bringing things into their space, making the world seem interesting and telling them about things they might not have heard about. There's also a lot of listening to them to see what they're interested in, and then thinking, oh, we've got a game about that, or we've got a book about that. Or there's a television series we could watch, you know. So there's a lot more of that when they're younger, although that definitely still happens."
HAYLEY

❝ I feel like my role is to make sure that there's enough variety and enough experiences available to her. I think that's the most important thing." **LIANNE**

❝ I definitely do see that our role as parents is to introduce them to things. Not saying, 'This is what you're going to be interested in', but to introduce them to the world, to take them places, to introduce things to our home that might be interesting to them. At the moment I'm gathering up a list of good YouTube channels that have lots of interesting engineering and STEM [science, technology, engineering, and mathematics] stuff in, so that I can create a playlist. When we're all feeling a bit like 'Oh, what can we do?', we can just put that on."
JAYNE

❝ When they were younger, my role as a facilitator was much more prominent, and I felt that I wanted to expose them to as much of life as possible so that they could choose or discount avenues. Over the years this has looked like: wanting to learn musical instruments, languages, politics, animation, art, travel, philosophy, journalism and so much more. They are young adults now, but I still view us as a home-educating family and I feel that my role is to listen and support in a broader, more emotional sense. I'm always an unconditional supporter of them and of their passions." **NICOLA**

Learn alongside them

Don't be afraid to admit what you don't know and to learn alongside your children. By around the age of 10 and 11, both my sons had a level of knowledge of geography and history that far surpassed mine. They acquired facts at an incredible pace, and I remember standing in the kitchen one day, furtively doing some online research on my phone just to keep up, and thinking how ironic it was that I ever thought I would be leading the way. I quickly gave up on trying to pretend I knew more than I did because it served little purpose, and was a lost cause anyway. I still often look up things they've talked about just out of interest and so that I can keep up with the conversations, but I freely share both my ignorance and my willingness to learn. They are endlessly patient with me and happy to fill in the gaps that many years of school and life failed to fill. So show them what it means to be an open-minded lifelong learner, and let them enjoy teaching you.

Prioritize conversation

Most of us love to talk about the things that are important to us. So open your ears and heart to whatever comes along, whether it's fashion design, gaming, dog training or politics, because you may well find that conversation becomes the bedrock of your children's learning. The beauty of conversation is that it serves so many wonderful purposes. It allows us to connect with our children while also learning about them and what matters to them, and appreciating all that they're learning. It helps them to clarify their thoughts, share their enthusiasm and hear other perspectives. And a conversation often allows an idea to take on a new form, to change course or transform into something entirely different.

> I tried to listen and be interested in what they were interested in, even if it wasn't interesting to me, because that allowed them to open up to

more conversation. My son went through a period of really liking cars, so he'd watch *Top Gear*. And my first thought was probably, oh I don't want to watch car programmes. And then I'd watch it with him and he'd explain stuff to me, and it'd be really interesting because he was making it more interesting for me. So I think it was trying to stay curious and open-minded. And accept that just because it's something I think I'm not going to be interested in, I might be surprised." HAYLEY

Strew about potential things of interest

I have never been quite organized enough to say that I intentionally strew, although when my children were younger, I would often put out things we hadn't looked at in a while. I know people who do intentionally strew, and it's a great low demand way to keep the environment interesting. You can set out anything you think your child might find interesting, from games to craft materials. Just arrange them invitingly somewhere your child has easy access to, then let your child explore in whichever way they choose. Don't insist or try to explain how things are done, and watch out for where your motivation lies. If you think it will be fun and you have zero expectations, then strew away. If, on the other hand, you find yourself gutted that your children don't pick up the science experiment you strategically set up on the table, you may want to take a breather.

> I was seeing what made them tick, what their passions were. I loved strewing, just leaving things out for them to discover, and it really fulfilled my creative parenting side." NICOLA

I love the way that Hayley describes how ingrained the process of bringing interesting things to each other has become in her family:

> In the beginning, when he was little, I'd put out some kind of little scene on the dining room table or different-coloured liquids, or something. But I really tried not to have expectations about that

or to get annoyed if they didn't take part. I feel like the strewing is both ways now they're older. They're forever coming and saying, 'Oh Mum, I think you'd really like this', or they'll send me a video. My son's got watch lists of YouTube videos for every member of the family that he's collected. I think the habit of wanting to share things you've discovered that you think somebody else will like just builds and builds." HAYLEY

Help shift the gears

A key part of our role is to notice when things are feeling stuck and to see what we can offer to help shift gears. Whether your child feels bored or the mood just seems a bit low, sometimes a small suggestion can be enough to create a big shift in the day. When we make a suggestion, it's helpful that our focus is on our child's well-being and not on getting them to do anything in particular. When your child is relaxed and feeling good about life, the doing will flow far more easily, so invest your energy in helping them reach that place.

For children who have a particularly strong need for autonomy, such as (but not only) PDA children, it's extremely easy for us to cross a line without realizing it. A genuinely innocent suggestion may cause them to feel under demand, even when the idea does in fact appeal to them. If your child gets anxious when they feel something is expected of them, time spent exploring this territory and tuning into their responses is time valuably spent. And the less focused you are on outcomes and expectations, the easier your communication will be.

Help to create structure

One of the many benefits of learning beyond school is that you can create a structure that works for everyone. Some children may prefer to have quite a defined week with a timetable of their activities, and days that always have a similar rhythm to them. Others can feel constrained by this, and may thrive on being more spontaneous. Helping our children have the kind of structure that works for them is a big piece in this, and is also a wonderful way for them to learn about themselves. So, rather than assuming we know what they need, we can figure it out with them, helping them understand what needs to be tweaked or adapted. You might find that your child goes through different phases and tries out different things.

One of my children loves to do lots of activities, but can find the scheduling challenging. Every so often, they ask me to help them figure out how they can shift things around so it all works better. They're learning how to organize their time, where their limits are and how much downtime they need – all valuable tools for the future. Another of my children used to regularly draw up a strict schedule to follow and spend a long while making it look pretty. They'd follow it for a few days, then find it too rigid and boring and cast it aside. After much trial and error, they now have a good understanding of how they like their days to be and what feels healthy and balanced for them. If they feel like they're missing something – like exercise, quiet time or adventure – they'll suggest ways to make that happen.

Many families find that they naturally fall into a structure based on activities that punctuate the week. And, as they find what works well for them, downtime and rest take on more importance. Parents often tell me what a revelation it was to actually plan time to rest and recharge into their days. So after a busy morning, everyone might naturally want a quiet afternoon. Or if a couple of days involve socializing with lots of other people, everyone might be ready for a more gentle day at home.

If you're finding it hard to figure out a balance between doing things out of the house and spending time at home, try planning for something small while being open to it becoming something bigger. Going out to jump in some puddles, a quick bike ride, a stroll to the shops – some of our best days have begun with something simple and then felt like a small adventure as they've unfolded in unexpected ways. This is particularly good if you have a child who, for whatever reason, isn't keen on big days out or who gets anxious. Rather than you having a fixed plan in your head, let them choose whether to head home or continue the adventure. For us, this is also a wonderful exercise in letting go of expectations and being present to what unfolds.

> We have certain cornerstones in our week. So there are things that we've now found that we really love going to and that work for me and for the children. So we go to a social group on a Wednesday, and a music group on Thursday. And then Friday tends to be more of a chill-out day, because the local market is on. So we sort of know how the week's going to flow, but other than that, we tend to leave it quite open." JAYNE

> She used to want me to give her a timetable and ask for something that looked like a school day and I'd be delighted. I'd love nothing more and I'd feel really good about myself. So I'd print something off, like worksheets. Then she wouldn't want to actually do the timetable, and I'd be upset because I'd made all that effort. Then we'd argue about the timetable. I realize now that she wanted structure and that's what she was used to but she didn't need those activities. At the time, she wasn't in a good place mentally, so a whole empty day probably felt quite overwhelming for her. It probably sounds negligent to not be structured all the time because that's what we think good parenting is. I learned not to structure the whole day but just to make some suggestions. Now I check in, and rather than pressuring her to plan the day, I'll see if she needs anything. Sometimes she'll have her day all mapped out and she'll tell me what her plan is. Sometimes she needs me to come up with a couple of ideas. I test the water. I might make a suggestion and pick up on how that goes. I know her so well now that I can tell how much she needs from me." RHONDA

Beware of over-planning

There can be a tendency in the beginning to want to over-structure the days, because downtime makes us feel anxious, and we might think our children need to be as busy as they would be if they were at school. But even if our children are on board with all of the plans, lack of downtime can leave everyone feeling depleted and grumpy. So, while we may feel pleased with ourselves for successfully filling up a whole day, we may also be missing out on rest time and on space for our children to feel into what they need. Don't feel like you need to let go of everything, but if your children are resistant to some of your plans, see if they would prefer to have more relaxed time in their days. Giving our children plenty of free, unstructured time allows them to get creative and for new ideas to develop.

> I never know what the day is going to hold. And I know that might be uncomfortable for a lot of people, but actually the days always turn into something amazing. You learn to go with the flow. When you have a plan, it can be quite limiting because you shut down opportunities to go in directions that you didn't even think of. My child might express something, and in my mind, I think it would be cool if we took that and did it in a particular way. But they might be thinking something completely different. We don't do it intentionally, but we often don't realize that we're not giving them the space to see where they want to go. We need to pause and ask them what their thinking is, understand where they're going, and then walk along with them."
> CLAIRE

> We used to struggle a lot with getting out of the house. To make this work, I have to be really flexible. So when there are these moments where she's suggested something, I've got much better at just paying attention and using the momentum of that. I just have to capture the enthusiasm and get in the slipstream. It's liberating and joyful, and trusting that your child's inherent intelligence is at work allows for a strong connection. Why have adults decided that children can't

possibly know what they want to do? Why do we think we always have to steer it?" DONNA

Help them regulate and reconnect

You will also be helping your child through the emotional ups and downs of life. Even when they have the freedom to plot their own path, they'll sometimes get frustrated and fed up, or feel bored and listless. If your child finds it hard to self-regulate, you may well find that things start to shift as they explore their autonomy, and the work you do in Part 2 will help you both cultivate tools that help you find regulation and connection in difficult moments.

> She's done a lot of reflecting on her feelings, which she didn't have space to do before because her feelings were so overwhelming. Now she can access the parts of herself that feel vulnerable and fearful. Things may still sometimes overwhelm her, but she can reflect on it afterwards and she'll be able to talk about it and look for the learning in it. What was the trigger? What was her nervous system trying to do? And what actually was the information that she needed? So she's got a kind of awareness of herself and her internal states that we just didn't have time to explore or unpack before." DONNA

Facilitate friendships and community

Your child's friendships and social life are likely to be high on your list of concerns about life out of school. And just like with learning, you'll probably find that you have a lot of conditioned thoughts about friendships that have their roots in school. School has normalized children spending all day with a large group of children the same age as themselves, so you may feel like you're failing your child if you can't provide a constant stream of good friends of their age. But although some children may thrive in this way, there's no evidence that this is what most children would naturally choose for themselves if they had the agency to decide. Children are as fantastically varied in their social needs as we adults are. Out of school, and with your support, your child can enjoy the level of social interaction and the kind of friendships that they need and find comfortable. With no pressure to fit in or be a certain way, your child has the opportunity to create authentic, healthy friendships in a way that works for them. (See Chapter 14 for ideas on how you can build a community for all of you.)

> At the beginning, my son found the social stuff really hard. I wasn't secure in it either, which means that he would have been picking up on that sort of anxiety too. Now he will go and play and be involved in things, but very much on his own terms. He doesn't feel any pressure to do that, which I really love. He does things as he wants to do them, and he can advocate for himself. He can get frustrated by things, but he will manage that himself, or he will let his friends, who are helpful friends, help him to do things." JAYNE

> The key has been to look at the children I have and to listen to what they say. Getting away from the 'shoulds', like assuming they have to join groups and only socialize with children their own age. S doesn't really go to any groups now, but he plays a lot of football so he sees kids at training. He's very happy. He likes to go to football games by himself all around the country, and he's having a great time, but it's more adults that he's talking with. He always found his own age group quite hard to be with. I think, like me, he prefers a good conversation. So he's having these incredible conversations with all sorts of people who love the same thing that he does. It's really wonderful that he hasn't felt the need to conform and try to fit in. Instead, he's going out into the world as himself and finding the people he can be himself with. G went to a STEM place and connected with three other children. They all love the same things and get on brilliantly. They meet up

quite regularly – organizing it all themselves. There are so many skills in maintaining friendships and I love how they take the lead." **CLAIRE**

Help them navigate the wider world

As your child grows, there will almost certainly be times when you need to help them understand what the next step could look like, and to bring your knowledge and research to the table. They might have a clear idea of the career or studies they'd like to do, in which case you may need to help them figure out and plan for GCSEs, college applications, job interviews or apprenticeships. Or you may be needed as a sounding board for different ideas as they figure it all out. I am often reminded of how our own deschooling never ends. One of my sons recently took some GCSEs and I found some old perfectionism around exams popping up every now and again. And when conversations revolve around potential future studies and careers, I often have to contain my own enthusiasm around particular ideas that come up and remind myself to stay curious and open-minded when I can't yet understand the appeal of others.

Am I doing enough?

This question is likely to drive you a little mad. What would enough look like? With no model to follow and no one else to tell you if you're doing it right, you'll never find a definition of 'enough' to soothe your mind. If you are attempting to respond to your children and meet their needs without taking over, while also looking out for your own conditioning, then you are almost certainly doing enough. The problem with this question is that it easily drives us to the kind of action that isn't at all helpful. The tension that propels us to do more can make the space feel less free and inviting to our children. So how about trying to find other questions that are easier to answer, such as 'Does this feel good?', 'Is my child happy?', 'Is there any way I can help them in their journey right now?' or 'Is there anything else I can bring to this that they would appreciate?'

There may well be times that life does feel a little boring or that you or your child feel in a bit of a rut. This could be the result of a child gaining confidence to do new things, or getting ready to spread their wings a little more. If you understand these moments simply as a natural part of the journey, you'll have the ability to bring a calm, creative mind to it. Rather than berate yourself for not doing enough, have some fun thinking about what else you might all enjoy. Check in with your child and see if you're on the right track, or test the water with a couple of suggestions.

Journal prompts

- Are there any other ways you could support your child in their interests? Think about the things they are naturally drawn to rather than the things you'd like them to choose!

- In what ways can you bring the real world into your home? And in what ways can you explore the world around you?

- How much structure does your week have? Does it feel right for everyone (including you)? If not, what shifts could you make?

Chapter summary

- There are lots of things that we can do to support our children, but these need to come from a place of trust and allyship, not from a place of worry or fear.

- There are no rules about what is needed of us. It will depend

- on many things, including our children's ages and interests, as well as how much support and company they need from us.

- We may often find ourselves out of our comfort zones, and it's okay to show them that we're always learning too.

- Meaningful conversations often serve as a cornerstone for learning. They help us understand our children's interests, build connections and learn together.

- Balancing structured activities with unstructured time is essential for fostering creativity and self-discovery. Recognizing when downtime is needed prevents burnout and allows children space to explore their own ideas and passions.

Chapter 6

Navigating technology

I was initially unsure of dedicating a whole chapter to technology and screens. It seems that everyone has a different opinion on this contentious topic, and it's hard to move for all the conflicting advice. But, when I think back to our early days and all the conversations I've had with parents since, there's no doubt that this is the place that causes the most worry when children come out of school and are given more freedom over how they spend their time. I can probably count on one hand the parents I've met who haven't at some point agonized over technology and their children's use of it. Gaming, social media, YouTube, absolutely anything that involves a screen – it all gets a bad rap and it's hard not to get caught up in the panic. 'Screen time' seems to have become equated with wasted time and inherent danger, no matter what the activity is that's taking place. And so, logic says that to be good parents and keep our children safe, we must impose limits. Nowhere do social conditioning and fear of the unknown come together to create quite such a perfect storm as with our children and technology.

With all the noise and pressure, we'd be forgiven for thinking that this is the one area where we need to forget about trust and autonomy. Or for believing that it's even okay for our relationship to take a hit given what's at stake. But I would make a case for the exact opposite. In this chapter, we're going to look at how nurturing our children's autonomy and our relationship with them is the best way to ensure that they stay safe and healthy online and offline. We're going to look both at how technology can be a happy and appreciated part of your lives, and how you can understand and work through any related fears or issues with your child.

Without school in the picture, the dynamics shift

How your child uses and interacts with technology can feel like a huge deal when they come out of school. There is a kind of double whammy that sometimes happens and can take parents by surprise. Not only is your child freer to choose what they do, but they are at home where the technology is. It's all further complicated by the fact that whatever your child is interested in, they will undoubtedly need to source much of their information online – not because they are addicted to anything, but quite simply because that's where it is. Add to this any expectations you might have had of how the days would be spent, your own internalized worries and concerns about what other people would think, and it's easy to see why it can all feel like picking your way through a jungle.

It's also true that when a child is free to make their own choices, the dynamics are likely to shift over time. We can't really compare a child who spends a large chunk of their days at school with relatively little autonomy to one who is free to interact with technology when they need. I remember when my sons used to arrive home after school. They would get straight onto Minecraft with a palpable sense of not wanting to waste a minute of their allotted time. That changed after leaving school. They still played Minecraft, but it tended to be either marathon sessions (and yes, I would get edgy), or none at all for weeks. Not having a set time or limit gave them the power to use the game in the way that worked best for them. And, it turns out, that wasn't at 5 pm every day for an hour and a half.

> " I've been on a bit of a crash course with screens. We used to have set times, like a couple of hours each day, and it was alright except that they were always asking for them and it felt like they were just waiting for that bit of the day. I get it now. If you make something that tempting and limited, it makes it more attractive." HOLLY

What is screen time anyway?

Before going any further, I'd encourage you to throw away the term 'screen time'. It covers such a multitude of activities and devices that it has no real meaning. If you see me on a screen, I am possibly reading the news or answering an email. Equally possible is that I'm texting a friend, organizing a trip somewhere, buying a child some new trousers or any number of other things. I'd find it patronizing if another adult referred to all this as my 'screen time'. And so it follows that it is patronizing to our children for us to lump all their activities together under this one overly general term. It makes it sound like we don't know or value what they're doing and have no desire to find out.

It took me quite a while to get beyond my fears around technology, and there was certainly plenty of fear, guilt and panic involved. But over the years, any worries have quietly fallen by the wayside, and technology and screens are interwoven into our children's days like they are into ours. They relax with them, connect with other people, learn, research and create things. Sometimes, like most people, they use technology to zone out, or because it's an easy solution to boredom, but they're pretty good at spotting when that happens.

The richness of technology

As our children get older, I appreciate how much richness technology has brought into our home and the myriad ways in which it facilitates me staying connected with their interests and with them. To illustrate this point, here are just a few of the activities that my children have used technology for fairly consistently over the last few years:

- research: geography, history, linguistics, politics, dog breeds, exercise routines, future careers, ecology, travel plans, recipes, martial arts – you name it, they've probably researched it
- learning languages
- watching/listening to songs in foreign languages

- researching the family tree
- researching maps and ethnic groups around the world
- researching for a coin collection
- reading the news
- learning guitar
- finding local dogs to walk
- doing geography quizzes
- playing Roblox (generally with friends)
- playing Minecraft (generally with friends)
- playing Star Stable (always with friends)
- gaming (mostly single-player strategy games)
- playing Mario Kart together on a rainy day
- watching documentaries, comedies, TV series, political satire
- drawing and craft tutorials
- graphic design programmes
- editing videos
- connecting with friends on social media.

Technology offers learning opportunities

The reality is that the learning opportunities available to our children online are phenomenal. Although there are lots of other ways to learn, little can beat the immediate wealth of information available to a curious mind online. For a child who is free to direct their own learning journey, it's an incredible way to explore and discover the world, far beyond the confines and limits of their family and culture. I recently found one of my sons looking a bit bemused. He explained that he had been searching for more information about a particular African leader. Ten minutes later, he found himself learning about a small town in Paraguay. He wasn't quite sure how he'd got there – he'd just followed the threads of his own curiosity, and that's where it had taken him. To some people, such random and exploratory learning may seem a bit pointless, but I've seen how the breadth of knowledge acquired in such a light and interesting way is astounding.

My other son loves languages and has many language books and flashcards. But nothing can compare to the wealth of ingenious ways that he has found to learn online – from language learning apps to gaming in a foreign language, watching films with subtitles on or, his favourite, singing along to videos of foreign songs on YouTube. We all get a lot of pleasure now attempting to follow along to songs in French, Polish, Korean, or whatever the language *du jour* is. My daughter, in her quest to get a family dog, has spent many hours researching dog breeds, calculating costs and watching dog training videos. She collated all her findings for me in a beautiful presentation that she created in a graphic design program.

If we're limiting, we're probably judging

I often wonder how we would have fared if I had attempted to limit any of that. How would it have looked if I said that two hours of technology each day was plenty? Would I have applied the same rules to researching the family tree or learning the guitar as I would to gaming or Roblox? What if they were connecting with one of their friends from Spain on Roblox? And is it okay to game if it's an accurately historical game? Would that make it more worthy? Who am I to judge anyway? And what about the needs for autonomy, competence and connection? How about if I did judge, but then they flitted intuitively between activities – as is often the case – doing something challenging and then relaxing a while with something else? The mind boggles!

Here, the easy flow between activities that use technology would be ruined if I attempted to judge or encourage. If one person is on their tablet for a while, they might be playing a game, but could just as easily be researching or learning Spanish. Another is as likely to be watching comedy on YouTube as reading about world politics. And another may be trading memes with their friend or deep into studying maps of far-flung places. We come back to the fact that, for the child, one activity is not more meaningful than the other. I've never asked, but I'm pretty sure they don't think, right, that's enough fun. I'd better learn something now. They just get on with what is appealing, and the change between activities is quiet and entirely unpredictable.

❝ My son loves gaming with people all around the world and he loves

researching. Over the years I've been absolutely amazed by how much he's learned from those video games. When he was little I would sit and try to help him learn how to do different things on Minecraft. Now he shares things with me. It might be the amazing music in a game or a video about the Egyptians. He spends a lot of time researching stuff behind the video games, especially if it's a history one. He's really knowledgeable about the world wars and he'll look at things like whether the games have accurately represented the technology at the time or if they've advanced it for the video game."
HAYLEY

> I never regulated screens and they have both dipped in and out of spending large amounts of time on screens, although neither of them is particularly attached to their phones. My daughter is an avid gamer and she has taught me to understand and not to make assumptions about something I know nothing about. She has a close community of friends online and is now studying game design at college, something which has come naturally from her passion for gaming." **NICOLA**

> For my youngest, Minecraft has added a new element to his love of architecture and he now designs the most complex structures. I remember in the second week of being out of school, he came to me and said, 'Mummy, I have a strange feeling inside me... I think I may be proud of the house I built in Minecraft.' He was starting to rebuild his self-confidence by spending his time doing something he was passionate about." **ANNIE**

> My children have tablets of their own and we used to have limits on them, but we don't now. The caveat of that is that my children are very regulated around it so there's never been an issue. We have parental controls and things, so they only have YouTube Kids, and we can block things. The reality is that YouTube exists and Google exists so we have to work on it together. I'm not anti-screens at all because I think they're an incredible tool, and I think our children need to know how to use them. My son really responds to things that

are gamified, and I understand that it's much more interesting doing maths in a game than on a worksheet. My daughter and I just had a conversation about how she wants to be a vet, and we talked about the things she'll need to study when she's older, and she's chosen to use BBC Bitesize to learn maths." JAYNE

Technology helps them stay connected

Technology provides children with spaces in which to connect with friends and with people who share their particular interests. It can also be a way for the family and siblings to enjoy time together. None of this means that they can't also connect offline. Later on in this chapter we'll talk about how we can help our children stay safe in their online interactions.

❝ My daughter pointed out that screens have been quite communal in our family. We have a lot of shows that we watch together and we play a lot of video games together. I don't play as much now, but I love to watch them play. One of my daughters lives away from home now, so she might join them all on Zoom." HAYLEY

❝ I didn't understand my daughter's relationship with social media and just assumed it was all bad and needed to be limited. But she is more astute than I could have imagined. We have conversations around it and she shows me what she does. It all revolves around her special interests and she gets a lot of connection and community through it. I've gone from feeling afraid to having the unexpected pleasure of seeing that she has found a community of people who love what she loves. I've learned to be a lot less judgemental about her choices. Giving them space is really important, and keeping the conversations open." RHONDA

Technology can be a safe space in a turbulent world

There's a tendency in our culture to blame technology for every conceivable problem with our children. Although it can certainly be problematic, such a sweeping approach also feels like a convenient way for older generations to avoid responsibility for the many ways in which modern life is quite hostile to young people. From stressful learning environments to environmental doom, lack of safe spaces and community, and a culture that places a higher value on people's superficial achievements than on how they are, there are myriad reasons why the offline world is playing its part in mental health crises. For a child who has anxiety, finds the world overwhelming or is healing from a stressful time at school, the online space can be a safe haven. In this case, when we stop judging and making assumptions that technology is the root cause and instead pay attention to how our children are, we are much better placed to support them. Rather than allowing their use of technology to create friction in your relationship, see if it can help you connect instead. Show a genuine interest in what they are doing, take them a cup of tea or a snack, sit with them if they are happy with that. Perhaps you can find gentle ways to use their online interest to connect with other people offline or inspire new conversations, or something you could do together.

> At one point, after my ex-husband and I broke up, my daughter was in severe autistic burnout. She just went into herself and that was her safe space and I had to let it all go. That was hard – I felt a lot of shame and like the worst parent in the world. But I also understood that this was partly what we all needed, a period of hibernation, and so I just trusted. We had three months like that. Then we came out of it and now there's much more of a balance, with days they use screens more and days they use them less. I notice that when they are regulated they don't need them so much." HOLLY

> I was never a gamer and I used to see it as a big red flag and something I had to stop her from doing. When I stopped judging her negatively, I realized she was using it to regulate and that it was helping her heal. Once I was able to see that, she felt like she could talk to me about it and explain to me that it was helping her. And I saw that she wasn't just passively scrolling. Some of the games she played were very creative. She was purposefully building things or in role-play games, or

one that was about designing according to a budget. I played games with her, and I was rubbish but it was really good for us to reverse our roles and have her telling me what to do. It helped her see that she could trust me and that I did really value and respect what she was doing." RHONDA

Online and offline, it's all real life

It seems like there is a fear that once children get a taste for life online, nothing will ever move them away from it and they will stop knowing how to engage in 'real life'. My experience is that life online and life offline is all real life and it is all constantly mingling and merging. Information and ideas have flowed into our lives from the online world, often translating into offline activities and vice versa. Online fantasy worlds became games in the garden, or inspired drawings and LEGO® builds. A book on micronations led to a deep dive online into micronations around the world, and then returned offline to inspire endless conversations in the kitchen. One particular favourite was Minecraft afternoons, where a couple of our children's best friends would come over and they would have a riotous afternoon laughing and playing online all in the same room. If we can get away from the belief that offline is somehow better than online, we can allow this rich cross-fermentation of ideas, fun and inspiration to flow.

Keeping our children safe and healthy – playing the long game

Of course, there will be many valid worries about how our children may be affected by technology, including exposure to content that is scary or inappropriate, toxic environments, cyberbullying, identity theft, predatory behaviour, catfishing and misinformation. Arbitrary limits may sometimes be appealing, but at best they give parents short-term relief, and we are in this with our children for the long game.

We certainly want them to be safe and healthy right now, but we also want them to know how to acquire the skills they need to always keep themselves safe and healthy. We want to help them work out how to move in the online world. We want them to be discerning about online friendships, be able to spot a toxic situation, and know when to walk away. We would like them to be aware of when they have got stuck and would rather be doing something else. So how can we go about keeping them safe and healthy within the context of trust and autonomy? I like to consider the following.

Is there a real fear, or are you just caught up in the noise?
It's important first to understand if we are caught up in the idea that screens are just bad, or if we have a genuine concern. I think my own reactivity in the beginning came from being hung up on the simplistic narrative that good parents limit screen time. My children were having a great time playing games like Minecraft and watching some fairly innocuous Minecraft-playing YouTubers. I could see that what they were doing was interesting, fun and challenging and, in fact, Minecraft happened to be brilliant for their reading and their maths. There was absolutely nothing wrong at all – it just made me feel like a bad parent! My shift began when I realized that the only way forward was for me to get curious. It felt like such a relief to give myself permission to sink into what they were enjoying and to nurture our relationship at the same time, rather than feel like it was almost my duty to be grumpy and disapproving.

Reacting to a generic fear about screens will do little for your child or for your relationship. When we make broad assumptions about how they are spending their time, they are likely to feel unsupported and mistrusted. Although our reaction may be based on concern for their well-being, we are more likely to alienate them and create conflict in our relationship, closing off the very communication channels that are so essential for helping them stay safe and well. Simply put, the more reactive we are, the less help we are.

So, if you're not quite sure what you're worried about, ask yourself what would happen if you just gave yourself a break and got curious. In Part 2 of this book there are lots of ideas and practices you can use to figure out where the fear is coming from, and to work your way through it.

Nurture their sense of self and their navigation system

The agency with which our children lead their lives offline will help them online. When we allow them to follow their navigation system and make choices that feel right to them, they become practised at checking in with their intuition, and knowing when a boundary has been crossed. When they have never been shamed into complying or following the crowd in order to feel worthy, they are less likely to do so online. When they have had the freedom to walk away from situations that feel disempowering or uncomfortable, to speak up when something feels unsafe and be taken seriously, and generally advocate for themselves and their values, they will feel more confident to also do this online.

I have been impressed many times by how my children handle situations online and their ability to self-advocate. Not so long ago, I watched as my daughter explained why a person in the game she was playing was flouting the rules and acting in bad faith against another player. After blocking this character, she penned a beautifully worded message to the moderators, explaining what had gone on and defending the wronged player. I was impressed by her intolerance for bad behaviour and her level-headed response. I have also noticed how alert they all are to the general mood of online spaces, and how comfortable they feel in them, just as they are alert to this in the offline world.

Help them be discerning

A self-directed child is used to doing their own research, often consulting multiple sources and working out how they feel about what they come across. They haven't been told that there is a right and a wrong or to take things at face value just because a person is older than them or looks and sounds knowledgeable. If all voices in the house are valued, including theirs, they will be used to knowing that there are many ways of looking at things, and that we don't always all agree. Help them nurture the ability to be discerning through conversations on topics they feel passionate about. Be curious about the information sources they use to find things out and who they trust. You might be surprised by their answers.

Tend the relationship

All that beautiful work you're doing to hold space for your child is so important now. The qualities you are cultivating in yourself, like trust, non-judgement and curiosity, will help you build and maintain a relationship in which your child knows that they can always come to you. Whether they regret making an online purchase, didn't get to the next level in a game, have experienced someone being unpleasant to them, wish they hadn't spent an hour on YouTube or have seen something that made them feel uncomfortable, they must know that you are, above everything else, their ally, and that you will always listen with compassion and curiosity.

Know and understand what they do

Different children will interact with different things online and in different ways, so understanding what your child does is key to knowing if there are any places you should be concerned about or in which you can support them. There's no point worrying about multiplayer shooter games if your child has absolutely no interest in them, or getting too riled up about social media if they only use it now and again to connect with close friends. Instead, take a specific interest in what your child does and who they connect with. Be aware of any particular difficulties they might have in this context, so that you can help them navigate if necessary. For example, if they struggle with ways in which other people communicate, this could be a good opportunity to help them understand nuances in conversation, or to help them set a boundary if they feel someone is treating them disrespectfully.

Talk openly about online safety

Taking away arbitrary limits doesn't leave a void. They are replaced by conversation, discussions, interest and involvement. For many reasons, including the age of your children, you may well have some restrictions in place around what your children can access or the devices that are available to them. Keeping the conversation open around these as your children grow older is a great way to ensure that there is an ongoing dialogue around online safety. If your children push for a new game that you're not sure about, be open to learning about it. If you're not comfortable with it, explain why to them. Encouraging these two-way conversations early on will set you up well for the future.

> We talk about online safety and what to do if anything comes up that makes them feel uncomfortable or upsets them and we just keep that dialogue open. We do the same with audiobooks. My daughter's now moving into books that are aged 9–12, so they're a bit older for her. So again, we have conversations about if something comes up in a book that you don't understand or that makes you feel uncomfortable or sad, and just keeping that conversation open." JAYNE

Suggest other things, but don't make it a competition

Many parents get worried about their children being on a device because it limits the time they spend doing other things. It's good to unpick this one a little before acting on it. First, think about whether you are worried because what they do is on a screen. Are they highly engaged in what they're doing and getting pleasure from it? Would you feel the same if they were spending the time reading or playing an instrument? We hear a lot about children being addicted to their screens, but no one complains about anyone being addicted to the guitar or to reading. It's certainly true that there are times when we all get stuck on screens, but be careful not to underestimate what they are doing for the sole reason that it's on a device. The next question is whether it is true that they are missing out on other things or that they are not getting enough exercise, or if there is some negative bias at work.

If you feel like you all genuinely need to get out or do something else, then go ahead and make a suggestion. But do it in a way that shows that you value what they're doing, and not as a way to drag them away from it. You could also try getting imaginative and think about ways that their online interests could inspire something you can all do together.

> When we decided to take the boys out of school we thought that getting a couple of iPads would be a great idea to help facilitate their learning. We downloaded Minecraft and other educational apps and just assumed they would flip-flop between them. But they were both smitten with Minecraft, and independently started their own race to learn as much as possible about it. They spent hours mastering the use of materials, different building styles, learning about different mods and coding. I found this all very triggering as I assumed using devices would be part of their learning and not all of it. At times like these, I would remind myself of the other activities we do together in any given week – forest school, swimming, skate park, play dates, comic drawing club, endless audio stories in the car, creating animation etc." ANNIE

Help them self-regulate

We all know how hard it is to pull ourselves away from certain things online. And some things are indeed designed with the sole intention of sucking us in. If we want our children to have the capacity to self-regulate, then we need to help them recognize when they've had enough and need a break. Again, although an imposed limit may seem like the only way to go, telling our children that they are incapable of self-regulating so we'll do it for them isn't necessarily going to help them develop the self-knowledge they need. And it may just give it all the allure of forbidden fruit. Set an example by being open and mindful about your own device usage, and let them know where you also struggle. Bring good humour to it – it's a part of life, and it's hard. I'll readily announce my frustration when I realize that I got hooked on something mindless, and my daughter and I often have a laugh about the weird things that have the power to lure us in. So let this be an ongoing conversation with no shame attached. Help them recognize and establish their own limits through talking with them and helping them in whatever way they need. You may find that they are extremely aware of when they feel like they've had enough and that, in the right context, they welcome your help.

❝ My daughter got a laptop for her 14th birthday. Before then we'd had a computer downstairs that had access to the internet and that was fairly unlimited. But suddenly, the laptop was a screen in the bedroom and we had this endless YouTube scrolling that went on for hours and hours, and my daughter was spiralling into quite a negative place. I was able to have some conversations with her about how she felt at the end of the day after watching all these YouTube videos compared to when she was downstairs watching videos about pottery or snakes or dog training, or any other kind of research. She could notice the difference but said she didn't know how to stop, so I suggested that I block YouTube from her laptop, although she could still use it downstairs. She agreed to that and hasn't asked for it back. So together we just put a limit around the thing that was causing difficulty." DONNA

❝ I don't put limits, but I ask them to be aware and keep track of the time in case they get sucked in. They have spent quite a lot of time online during certain periods and then, in fact, Max has said 'Oh Mum, you know I think we've been spending too much time online. I think we should have less now.'" EVA

❝ When they were younger, I would ask them how they were feeling, and I might remind them that when they last played on a screen for a long time they felt a bit rubbish. But I would never say, 'Well, you can't play it because you felt rubbish.' That would be like cutting off our communication channel, and I didn't want to do that. I wanted them to always be able to come and talk to me. They sometimes do no-screen-time challenges, when they think they're spending too much time online or on social media. When my daughter was about

15, she really liked Pokémon Go and noticed that her screen time was quite high. So she set herself the challenge that Pokémon Go would always be the highest app on her phone because that meant she was likely to have been outside while she was using her phone." HAYLEY

Some tips for living happily and safely with technology

- *Be interested and curious* about what your children do online.

- *Don't be dismissive or judgemental.* If you are mystified about their choice, try to understand some more.

- *If they're gaming, have a go with them.* Your child may well be delighted to show you what they're doing.

- *Have open conversations* about the potential hazards that exist online: safety, unreliable information sources, unpleasant characters, algorithms designed to suck us in.

- *Help them navigate difficult situations.*

- *Notice what their interests are online.* Maybe there are other, offline experiences you can suggest to help them delve deeper if they want to?

- *Stay attuned to how they are.* Are they happy and enjoying what they're doing, or are they bored and would welcome another suggestion? Are they needing to take some time out from a stressful world?

- *Make your relationship the priority* – always be a person they can come to.

- *Encourage them to trust themselves in life* and to always speak up when something feels wrong.

- *Observe yourself and the things that trigger you.*

Challenging my assumptions around gaming

Before I had children, I had some pretty firm views about video games. I had never gamed myself, and was completely ignorant about gaming, but I'd chosen to believe what I had heard and read. So, without ever looking at a game, I assumed that they were probably a waste of time – dulling young minds or influencing them negatively with violent content. Consequently, I was a bit challenged when, at around the age of 11, my son moved on from Minecraft to more sophisticated games. For a couple of years, he gamed a lot. By this time, I was deep into my deschooling process, so although I was frequently triggered by the many hours dedicated to gaming, I knew that this was more about me than about him. So I got curious. Instead of making concerned noises when he was at his computer, I would offer him a cup of tea or a snack. I sat with him and watched him play, and was amazed by his skill and by the sophistication of his games. I had a few goes myself while he patiently tried to help me navigate my way through some of the games he played. I was hopeless. I found the games incredibly complex – too much to read and too many rapid decisions to be made. I could also see that it was immensely gratifying and interesting for my son, and I started to really listen when he talked to me about his gaming.

He was playing games that tapped directly into his interests and expanding his knowledge of history, geography, economics and politics. He also delved into game design, teaching himself at home and attending a Saturday class for a while. We went to a gaming convention together, and besides having a great day, I got to see how this world lit him up. I knew absolutely nothing about it all, and he knew so much! As we wandered around, he explained the games, the companies and the technology to me. He even knew far more about all the retro games and devices from my own childhood. As a writer and editor at the time, I decided to write an article about gaming. I visited several gaming companies and interviewed people who were creating new games. I came home after these interviews, buzzing with excitement at the creativity involved. The whole experience of opening my eyes to what my son was interested in was humbling, and my assumptions were completely blown apart.

And so, I discovered that there was nothing mindless or dull about my son's gaming. He gamed because he enjoyed it and because it was fulfilling and challenging. He loved the storylines and the ability to be immersed in these fascinating worlds. There will certainly have been times that he chose to game because he felt bored or as a soothing antidote to a more confusing real world. In those times, gaming was a helpful resource for him. I think now how painful it would have been for him if I had been dismissive of his passion. Anecdotally, he rarely games now, although he still has a keen interest in the gaming world. The same interests that his gaming resourced are still very much alive.

Journal prompts

- Is there anything that triggers you about your child's use of technology?

- Are there specific fears or worries, or is it a generic fear?

- Can you see what your child is getting from their favourite online activities?

Chapter summary

- Children's use of technology when they leave school often leaves parents feeling anxious and under pressure to set limits.

- Technology offers incredible learning opportunities, and can be a great way to connect with friends and others with similar interests.

- The term 'screen time' is so broad as to be meaningless. If we are to support our children, we need to get away from generalizations and understand what they do online.

- Making our relationship with our children our top priority, and encouraging them to act with agency and discernment in their daily lives, will help our children maintain their boundaries and recognize when a person or environment doesn't feel right.

- We can help our children stay safe and learn to self-regulate by maintaining an open dialogue about how we use technology and the potential pitfalls.

Chapter 7

How fear keeps us going in circles

You've probably realized by now that unschooling is as much about you as it is about your child. It can be extremely hard to move beyond our old beliefs and patterns, so even when you truly believe that your child can learn and thrive out of school, you'll probably still have plenty of wobbly moments. Many parents are surprised by how often they feel anxious or fearful, and by the multitude of seemingly small things that spiral into panicky thoughts. They worry that their child will never engage with anything when they don't want to go to a museum. They get nervous about the future when their child watches something on YouTube they can't see the point of. They feel bereft when their child decides not to go to forest school any more. It's hard, but fear and the uncomfortable sensations that accompany it are an integral part of the deschooling journey. Why? Because every time we feel fear, we know that we have reached the edge of our comfort zone. In Part 2 of this book you're going to learn how to notice and work with those difficult moments, so you can start to move away from old beliefs and forge a new, freer path forward for your child and yourself. But before we do that, let's take a closer look at fear, and why this powerful emotion is likely to be both our biggest stumbling block and our greatest opportunity for learning and growth.

What is fear?

It may feel unpleasant, but fear keeps us safe. Have you ever mistaken a shadow for a lurking stranger, come across a huge spider or looked down from a great height? Before you had time to consciously register a thought, the physical sensations of fear will have kicked in. Rapid breathing, a surge of adrenaline, tense muscles, a knot in the stomach and a host of other symptoms act like warning bells to let us know we need to react, and quickly. This is the sympathetic nervous system – the fight or flight response – which is automatically activated when we are (or we think we are) under threat, giving us the capacity to respond immediately to the situation at hand without needing to waste valuable time on thinking things through.

Any rational thinking is secondary to getting ourselves to safety, so the prefrontal cortex (the part of our brain responsible for thinking, predicting and analysing) shuts down and lets the amygdala (the part of our brain responsible for processing emotions) take over the show. Those physiological changes that the amygdala triggers prepare our body to either confront the threat or run away from it (other responses include freeze or fawn). In this highly reactive space, our thinking becomes narrow and limited only to how we can solve the problem at hand. Once we have dealt with the threat or it has naturally subsided, our body returns to a state of equilibrium (unless we keep rehashing it in our minds – more on that later). Our prefrontal cortex comes back online, and the fight or flight response gives way to the parasympathetic nervous system – our more relaxed rest-and-digest state. It's a highly effective mechanism and one we owe our lives to. If we didn't feel fear, we would step happily into all sorts of risky situations, and probably not last very long.

Ways the brain interprets events to keep us safe

While most of us go through life thinking we are looking at an objective reality and making choices and decisions based on hard facts and evidence, nothing could be further from the truth. Unless we consciously choose to bring awareness to our days, our efficient, cautious brain just runs happily along on autopilot, constantly predicting the future and working out the best way to react to every situation we find ourselves in. Thousands of times a day, it assesses what's going on and what we need to do about it, and if it has an inkling that something is not quite as it should be, it lets us know through our nervous system. As we deschool, it's helpful to keep reminding ourselves of how the brain works, and all the ways it interprets life just to make sure we stay safe. It convinces us that things we are just imagining are real, that we're in terrible danger when we're not and it encourages us to exaggerate the small things. Although it's acting in our best interests, it certainly makes change harder.

We don't have to be in real danger to feel fear

We don't have to be in physical danger for our fight-or-flight response to be triggered. Being judged by a friend, your child not wanting to read, struggling to find time for yourself, maths! – these things and many others can set off those familiar sensations in the body. And no matter how much you tell yourself that everything is okay, your body still doesn't calm down because this system, which has evolved over thousands of years, operates without our conscious control. Although on the face of it none of these events are physically threatening, they are deeply connected to our survival and our selfhood. Fear of rejection, of the unknown, or of losing our autonomy – to our amygdala this is all the equivalent of being chased by a hungry lion. It's easy to understand why many aspects of leaving the school system can provoke extremely uncomfortable emotions.

We can't tell the difference between reality and imagination

To further complicate things is the fact that just thinking about something can bring about the same physiological changes in your body as when it's actually happening. It may seem obvious to us that reality and imagination are two completely different things, but our brain can't tell the difference between real threats and those generated internally by the neocortex. It responds to both the same way, and the more vividly we imagine something, the more real the experience seems to our brain. You might be happily engaged in some restful activity with your child, and then find your mind drawn toward your friend's negative comment, your child not reading, or the things you worry you're missing out on. Within moments, the light mood has shifted and you find yourself gripped by anxiety and stuck in rumination, even though absolutely nothing in your external circumstances has changed.

Negativity bias

Negativity bias is another of our brain's mechanisms that serves us well for staying safe but can easily ruin even the best day with our children. Negativity bias means that we place far more importance on negative events than we do on positive ones. From an evolutionary perspective, this is fantastic stuff because it gives us a heightened awareness of things that might be threatening. Research shows, for example, that if two equal things happen, a positive and a negative, we will almost certainly fixate on the negative, and are likely to see these potentially dangerous things as far riskier than they really are. If you were walking along the road and spotted something that looked like it could be a snake or a stick, you would be more likely to react to it as though it were a snake – just in case.

Negativity bias can be quietly sabotaging from a deschooling perspective, which is why we need to keep an eye out for it. I remember our early days of living without school. Everything would be flowing along happily until someone said they were bored, at which I would shift from feeling cheerful and satisfied with our lot to being gripped by the terrible thought that I was doing everything wrong. It didn't matter that we'd been out and about all morning, or that boredom was often followed by bursts of creativity. All my fearful mind could see was a bored child, proving that I was failing at this. Unable to just allow my child some time to figure things out, or to offer a sympathetic ear, I would come up with endless ideas to solve the boredom, and then feel even more frustrated as they were rejected. My child, sensing my frustration, would feel the pressure and resist even more.

Tunnel vision means we access limited information

Not only is it exceptionally easy for our fear response to kick in when, in fact, everything is fine, but when we are in fight or flight, we are also limited in how we receive and process information. Remember how children can't learn if they're anxious? Well, the same applies to us when we're in fight-or-flight. When we're in the grip of fear, we acquire a kind of tunnel vision where our brain can only access the most readily available information, so we have no access to new and creative ways of thinking, or, importantly, to our children's experience and perspective. This means that our responses are also limited.

We are hard on ourselves

Because we are hyperfocused on what is wrong and what we need to do about it, we tend to be judging and self-critical. Self-compassion often goes out of the window when we are fearful. We are far more likely to be chiding ourselves for getting it wrong or telling ourselves we have to do better. And that increases our discomfort.

We miss the richness of the present moment

Once a fear has been activated, if something doesn't fit our narrative, we're likely to miss it completely. I remember how, for a few weeks after my children left school, and filled with some pervasive fear around maths, I insisted my eldest son spend half an hour a day on an extremely dull maths workbook. I would feel frustrated because he didn't want to follow the methodologies that the book explained, wanting instead to create his own ways to solve the problems. I was so focused on him completing the daily two pages (or whatever goal I had set) that I couldn't see the creativity he was bringing to it or how he was trying to make this tedious task more interesting. Nor could I appreciate that he wanted to experiment and didn't even mind making the whole chore harder. I missed it all because my entire focus was on calming my fears around maths.

Patterns from the past keep us stuck in the same place

In its quest for efficiency, the brain is constantly creating habits and patterns, and it uses these to help process new information and make quick judgements. While this is essential for us to function effectively, it also means that most of our reactions to life are based on patterns created long ago. The same situations trigger the same feelings, which trigger the same reactions and the same words, often eliciting from our child the same reaction and the same words. It might feel like we are incapable of doing it differently, but this is the brain running automatic circuits.

When we react to life and our children from an old pattern, chances are that our reaction is not the best option. It may be the one that momentarily gives us the most relief or soothes our discomfort. Or it may be the one that other people think is right, or the one we are most used to, even though we kick ourselves for it later. The problem is that this old way of meeting our needs might not have much to do with our child right now – we're applying our past experiences to the present moment. And when we react from old patterns, we get even further away from where we think we should be, making us feel disheartened and even more reactive. So we go round and round in circles, ruminating over things we can't seem to solve, and simply watching the gap, between how we think things should be and how they actually are, get bigger.

Keeping the stress response active

Once a threat has passed for other mammals, typically they shake out the adrenaline and their system returns to normal. We, on the other hand, keep all that tension in our bodies and add a few more layers. It only takes 90 seconds for the chemistry of a stress response to run its course through the body. But we tend to dwell on things long after they've happened, and each time we relive the event in our mind, we reactivate the stress response, as though it were happening again. In doing this, the grooves of those neural pathways deepen and our habits become even more ingrained. And so, an event that creates a response of shame, anger or worry makes its way into our wiring as we relive it over and over, perhaps over days, years, and sometimes over a lifetime.

So what exactly are we scared of?

Fear of the unknown
Taking your child out of school can feel like a gigantic, blindfolded leap into the unknown, and our brains hate the unknown. After all, who knows what dangers and threats may lurk in places we're not familiar with? Just as soon as we open our minds to the possibility of something new, we find ourselves going over all the potential problems and reaching for evidence from the past, present and future to convince ourselves that stepping into uncharted waters could be a terrible idea. There may be all sorts of things that cause sleepless nights, from family members who aren't on board with the idea, to the financial and practical implications of changing jobs, or what it will mean for our children's futures. Better the devil you know, says the brain, triggering that cascade of uncomfortable sensations in its quest to keep us safe.

Once we start feeling that discomfort in the body and catastrophizing over all the things that might go wrong, it can feel like a much better idea to stick with the status quo than to risk the unknown. There is something understandably reassuring about school and the idea (however tenuous) that if our child follows a set path for a set amount of time, their future will be secure. Even when your child is struggling within the system, to leave all illusion of certainty behind and embrace something you may have never seen in action before is no small feat. I talk to many parents who took their children out of school after several difficult years, and who now kick themselves for waiting so long. At the time, though, the unknown felt like such a terrifying and lonely prospect that it wasn't until the fear was outweighed by the real distress of their daily lives that it felt safer to leave than to stay.

> My daughter was adamant about trying home education, but for some reason, my husband and I really focused on the negatives. 'Will you have any friends?', 'Will it be so easy to go to university if you want to?', 'What will everyone think?' It's like we were trapped in this kind of conditioning and too scared to take the leap. It's like I knew in

my heart that there was something better on the other side, but I felt like nobody around us understood. I had this fear that we'd be missing lots of positive opportunities and the community. And also because my daughter seemed to do the academic stuff so easily." HAYLEY

❝ My main concern was having community and continuity. As far as the learning, I totally trusted that she would learn what she needed to learn. I just about skimmed through at school. I didn't enjoy it and I didn't learn much from it. So, in a funny way, I think that freed me up from a lot of worrying." LIANNE

Fears rooted in our own childhoods
While many of the fears that show up as you're deschooling will ostensibly be about learning and about your child, you may well find that deeper fears of your own are also being triggered. Some parents get edgy when everyone isn't busy all the time, because their own self-worth is bound up in striving and being productive. My panic about my child being bored almost certainly triggered some old fear of my own about me not being enough and needing to do better.

It's normal that this new path challenges old patterns of insecurity and vulnerability, many of which we'll have lived with for most of our lives. Sometimes there is so much discomfort that people think their journey out of school just isn't working, or that they or their children are not cut out for this. But the discomfort is invaluable because it points us to the patterns that no longer serve us. As children, we all create ways to respond to the world that we believe will keep us safe. Depending on our environment and our caregivers, we might have learned that to be accepted we had to be compliant, or that to escape criticism we needed to strive to be perfect. Perhaps in a loud family we had to shout to be heard, or maybe we learned that our voice didn't matter, so it was better to stay quiet and small. Perhaps we became people-pleasers, and have placed appeasing others above meeting our own needs. Over time, we're likely to have repeated these patterns so often that they have become well-worn neural pathways, meaning that by the time we're adults, they're pretty much running on automatic pilot.

The core beliefs we have about ourselves and our own worthiness and place in the world will greatly influence the kind of stories we tell ourselves when things don't seem to go to plan with our children. When these fears come up, our days can easily become a haze of 'shoulds' with nothing quite making the mark. Here are some common beliefs about ourselves that might get triggered as we deschool:

- I need to be approved of.
- I have to be productive to be valued.
- I need to do everything perfectly.
- I have to prove my worth.
- I mustn't be angry/needy.
- I can do everything myself.
- It's up to me to make sure everyone is always okay.

Other people's scrutiny

The weight of other people's scrutiny and judgement when you choose a less-travelled path can add to the likelihood of your own patterns getting triggered. If you come from a background of being compliant, not ruffling feathers or needing approval, it may be extremely challenging for you to go against the status quo, even when you believe it's in your child's best interests. Many parents struggle, for example, with the knowledge that some people don't approve of them taking their child out of school. They are then likely to have a strong need to prove that everything is going well, and may be easily triggered when life doesn't look like they think it should, or when they have nothing to prove their child's learning.

> My challenges in the beginning were around feeling like it was okay to be doing what we were doing, and to have the courage and confidence to feel like our decision was valid. Not all our family were supportive about us taking them out of school. It's an ongoing struggle for me to know how to frame it for other people when they ask about it, and I

always end up listing the activities our children do. For me, it's been a challenge to question and challenge my own upbringing, my cultural conditioning and my own judgement and approval. Perhaps it's impossible to get away from that totally. It's always an external thing that triggers it, like chatting to a friend whose children are at school. And then I wonder if I should be thinking about that. My dad, who was a headmaster, is quite progressive and interested in alternative schools. So I had an ally, which gave me a lot of courage and confidence, and what I knew from my psychology degree and my research." EVA

Sitting in uncharted waters

Once we have taken the leap, it may be that some of the fears we had simply don't materialize. We might have thought we would get a lot of judgement from other people, but find they are helpful and supportive. We may find that our worries about work or logistics were unfounded, or that it's all less problematic than we had feared. Most likely is that none of it feels quite like we thought it would feel. Perhaps the most surprising thing that parents discover is that although the idea of leaving school can feel radical, the daily reality of it is far from radical. Your child now being at home with you is likely to feel both extremely normal and wildly unsettling, and it's here, in this odd transition space, that you find that all your ideas around learning and parenting are challenged in ways you had never imagined. The ideas you had planned to fill the weeks with probably don't go as smoothly as you had hoped. Your child may well not respond how you thought they would to your suggestions or engage with life in the way you envisaged. You might have imagined you would feel relaxed and joyful, but find that you're on edge a lot of the time.

If mainstream education is about attempting to make things certain, then self-directed education is about embracing that it is okay not to have all the answers. And if we want to accompany our child so that they can be their whole selves in this world, we have no choice but to learn to quieten the fears. Every time we react from fear or worry by trying to pin our children's journeys down and make everything feel certain, we risk derailing their journey.

> My children decompressed within a week and I could see the benefit in them immediately. They were no longer ill. They slept better and longer. They had energy and enthusiasm for the day ahead and their smiles returned. But it took me a long time to get over the narrative that children should be in school. I had a lot of guilt, even though I was loving it. I kept wondering if I should be doing more or if someone was going to come and check. I really pushed myself at school and I was quite academic, so it was always important to me to try to be the best and to always get A grades. So I had 40 years of conditioning to undo." **NICOLA**

> I think I felt immense pressure about their future and well-being and that their education was all my responsibility. That was overwhelming, especially as I was looking at it in a very schooly way. When they weren't doing it the way I felt was good enough or giving me the answers I needed, I felt like I'd failed. I felt a lot of anxiety about the situation, and I know that made me irritated towards my children. Often my focus was on what they weren't doing, but I know now it was all about my fears." **CLAIRE**

How does fear hold us back?

If we don't spend some time intentionally unravelling our fears, they will continue to come up for us in some guise or another, over and over again, diminishing our ability to hold space for our children and undermining their learning journey.

> The biggest challenges were around me relearning what learning means. I couldn't decide what this work looked like or what our lives would look like. There was panic at first about falling behind, and the fear of never catching up. In the beginning, we made timetables and

tried to structure the day, but that stressed us even more. We had to find our own rhythms. At each point, I had to let more stuff go until I got comfortable with trusting the process. Some of it was intuitive and some of it was just noticing that the days I wasn't stressing went better. So we needed more good days to figure out what we wanted to do and how we would be." DONNA

Fear stops us from sitting with possibility

When we are fearful, we tend to make assumptions about how things are going to work out, often reaching for the worst-case scenario. I remember when my children were small, and every time I could hear an argument brewing, I would quickly jump in because I 'knew' it would just get bigger. It took me a while to realize that my own deep aversion to any kind of conflict tended to make everything worse. I started to resist jumping in as an unwelcome peacemaker and held back. Nine times out of ten, they would resolve the problem themselves, bringing all sorts of sophisticated negotiating skills and often ending in hugs. Me intervening unnecessarily was stopping them from exploring other ways to approach the situation.

> I didn't think I would teach but I thought I would be really clever and just introduce topics and inspire them, like, 'Boys, look, this is the largest country in the world!' and they'd say, 'Wow, Mummy, thank you.' But they're just like, whatever, not interested. That made me panic more than anything. It was that classic thing of just trying to get the learning into them somehow. Despite listening to hours of podcasts and reading, I still went there. It's like a classic; you just can't help yourself." ANNIE

Fear stops us from seeing the process and fixates us on the outcome

Until we have built the capacity to sit with difficult emotions, our desire will always be to head for the solution. Unable to explore nuances or be open to other perspectives, our nervous system will push us to make things happen before they are ready to happen or to try to force outcomes. We will miss the most valuable part of self-directed learning, which is watching the process itself unfold.

Our pushing increases our child's resistance and we go around in circles

When we try to make things land before they're ready, we'll almost certainly be pushing against our child, or rushing their journey. Their logical response to this is most likely to be resistance, probably making us push even harder, and on it goes.

Our child internalizes our fears as proof that they are doing something wrong

In Chapter 4, we talked about how fear interferes with how we hold the space. If our children notice that their behaviour causes us distress, they may internalize the same thoughts and patterns that we ourselves are grappling with. If we don't unpick our worries, it's easy to simply project them onto our children.

Our child tries to soothe our fears by putting our needs before their own

Some children may try to appease their parent rather than resist. On the surface that may look like success and their compliance may well soothe our worries, but it won't help us understand our children or help them learn to move through life in a way that feels coherent.

> When she first came out of school, she was unable to engage in anything that looked like learning. She did a few things I gave her and all any of it did was temporarily calm me down. We have a lovely relationship, and I think she was doing it for me, to soothe me." RHONDA

Welcome discomfort!

The transition period can be a profoundly uncomfortable time. We have chosen to step out of one way of doing things, but we haven't quite worked out the new way yet. And until this new way feels just as familiar as the old way, our minds will keep trying to drag us back to the stable ground of the past and those old automatic patterns. It often isn't until we take our children out of school that we even become aware of how deep our conditioning goes. As we'll see in the next chapter, the issue isn't so much about whether we have fears or not – we all do – it's about how willing we are to engage with them.

Mirror neurons and helping your child self-regulate

If you have a child who is easily overwhelmed or who struggles to self-regulate, the work you do and the mindfulness tools you learn over the next few chapters will be as valuable to them as they are to you. Our own ability to self-regulate has a profound effect on our children and the patterns that they build in moments of challenge or conflict. A lot of this is explained through mirror neurons, a set of neurons in the brain that fire not only when we perform an action, but also when we *observe* someone performing an action. When we watch someone ride a bike, for example, the same mirror neurons fire in our brain as if we were riding a bike ourselves.

This occurs with facial expressions and tone of voice as well. When we are confronted with someone who is angry – strained voice, furrowed brow, narrowed eyes – the mirror neurons associated with anger fire in us. The same happens when we observe someone who is anxious, crying or laughing. In a very literal sense, mirror neurons allow us to feel what others are feeling. They are key to our survival – they help us understand when someone needs our help, and they let us know when someone is a threat.

The brain picks up and registers the signals on people's faces faster than it can process what they're saying. Our children's mirror neurons are highly active from when they are born, and a newborn baby can only see as far as their mother's face, because that's all they need to be attuned to – how their mother is feeling. So, if we are trying to keep calm but the emotions on our face signal anger or irritation, our child is far more likely to feel and respond to that. Our dysregulation, however it manifests, is highly likely to trigger similar feelings in our children (just as our children's dysregulation can be highly triggering to us).

Equally, if we are calm, thanks to mirror neurons, we automatically help our children to regulate their emotions. Our voice and demeanour communicate to them that everything is okay, that no matter what has happened, nothing is out of control and they are safe. This is immensely powerful. It also sends the message that we are unconditional in our support, and that we can hold them compassionately in their most dysregulated place. And we are showing them that it isn't always easy but it is possible to hold one's ground even when those around are dysregulated. Over time, and with our example, they will develop their own strategies for doing this.

Journal prompts

- Make a list of the things that most worry you about your child not attending school, or about them having more autonomy over their journey.

- Are these rational fears?

- Do you notice what deeper fears about yourself might be triggered?

Chapter summary

- Even when parents believe in their child's ability to thrive outside traditional schooling, their doubts and fears will cause many anxious moments.

- The purpose of fear is to keep us safe. It triggers our body's fight-or-flight response, activating uncomfortable physical symptoms so that we take action. The fears we have about our children often trigger deeper fears about ourselves.

- The brain can't distinguish between real threats and imagined ones, so it responds in the same way to both. This can lead us to overreact to situations that challenge our sense of safety or certainty.

- Fear narrows our focus, limits creative thinking and increases self-criticism. It shifts our attention away from the present moment, and rushes us towards solutions, often increasing resistance in our children and sabotaging the space.

- Being aware of our fears enables us to become familiar with our old stories and patterns.

Part 2

The four steps to freedom

If unschooling ourselves was just about understanding the theory, it would all be simple. But, of course, it isn't simple. At the end of Part 1 we talked about how fear tries to hold us in old patterns and prevent us from embracing the new and unknown. Undoing those old patterns takes time and focus, and relies on you being willing to engage with all the little triggers as they pop up each day. In Part 2, you'll find four key steps to help you navigate those uncomfortable moments. Rather than reacting to them, you'll learn to become aware of the triggers as they arise, observe them with compassion and curiosity, and then respond from a new, more conscious place. And you'll come to appreciate that every worry, fear or challenging moment is also an invitation to growth, learning and connection:

- Step 1: Pause!
- Step 2: Be kind
- Step 3: Be curious
- Step 4: Engage

Chapter 8

Step 1: Pause!

So how do we get free of this programming that wants to keep us stuck in the same old place? How can we convince our brains that we would like to get beyond the limits of school-style learning, that we want to relax into our days with our children and feel joyful rather than nervous? How do we get the message across that we're ready to step into uncharted waters? It's rarely enough to know and understand the theory. Unless we dig deep, our old patterns will still kick in to trigger us into staying safe. It takes courage to choose a lesser-trodden route, and then it takes intentionality to keep moving forward and using each of these uncomfortable moments as a place of growth. Instead of ignoring, running away or shutting down the triggers when they arise, in the next few chapters we're going to learn how to pause, zoom in with compassion and curiosity, and then choose a different way forward. To help you navigate this, this and the following three chapters explain this process of moving through the discomfort in four mindfulness-based steps.

Our work in this chapter is to learn to catch the trigger before it heads down the usual path. But first, let's look at some common things that are likely to put our nerves to the test when we choose not to send our child to school, and then we'll see how we can apply 'Step 1: Pause!'

What triggers us

When we are still in the leap-of-faith stage, many of our triggers are likely to be around learning and what our child does.

No proof of learning
If you're used to seeing the tangible results of learning, you may well find yourself worrying that nothing is happening. Your child might decide to write something down or to create something because they enjoy that, but they are highly unlikely to write you an essay about what they've been delving into or create a PowerPoint. Given that schools are true production lines of learning evidence, this can be disconcerting. And even if you know the learning is happening, how can you prove that to other people if there's nothing to show?

Activities you can't see the value in
Your child has lots of opportunities for interesting outings and activities, and you envisioned them choosing to spend their days on things that look creative and educational. So why, you wonder, do they choose activities that seem to have no value?

Not wanting to take up your suggestions
When you have a clear idea of what a healthy and interesting life looks like, it's challenging when your child doesn't follow your lead, particularly if you've put a lot of time and thought into it. You buy lots of fabulous art stuff and set it all up in the kitchen, but after a half-hearted attempt at something ends in frustration, your child wanders off, leaving you to paint by yourself. You find a special interest group they could join that seems like the perfect fit, but after the usual to and fro of emails about times and dates etc., your child has no interest whatsoever in going. You can see they want to do things, but they won't let you help them.

Time with screen-based activities

Pretty much everything you ever read about screens is negative, so every time they do anything screen-related, you feel like a terrible and negligent parent. This is amplified to the power of a hundred if the chosen activity is YouTube or a game that seems to have no educational value at all. Now, you think, not only are they on screens but they are also wasting time, and you ask yourself if you can really trust them to make good choices.

Not wanting to go out

Some children love to be out and about, and some will steadfastly resist their parent's pleas for a walk or a bike ride. This is hard because not only do we worry about exercise and fresh air, but when our children are young, we may also rely on them going out to get our own daily dose of nature and vitamin D. The more you suggest, the tenser it gets, until suggesting a walk turns into a battle of wills in which everyone loses. You feel the world getting smaller and panic a bit more, and they resist a bit more.

Boredom

They keep telling you they're bored, but don't want to do anything you suggest. You feel hopeless and wonder where it's all going so wrong. Why isn't this working? What else do you need to do? Depending on the day, you either jump into action, finding more things to suggest, or descend into despair. You wonder if your child has enough initiative for self-directed learning.

Giving up

Your child never seems to stick at anything. After an initial flurry of enthusiasm, every new interest quickly loses its shine. Plans get abruptly abandoned and half-finished projects get pushed to the back of cupboards. You worry they'll never get anywhere if they can't stick at anything.

Falling behind

Everything is ticking along just fine and your child seems happier than they've been in a long time. Then a friend tells you what their (similar-aged) child is doing at school. You feel a pang of worry and shame. Your child probably doesn't know anything about that, and you question everything you're doing. What if your child is falling behind? How will they ever catch up again?

When our reactions come from a place of fear

When we're unable to press the pause button on these fears, we have a tendency to hijack our child's learning journey to make it all look more palatable to us, bypassing process and thundering on to outcome. If we're highly triggered, this might look like us getting frustrated or upset, trying to convince our child to do something they don't want to do, or even getting into an argument with them. Other times, our response can be more subtly coercive, and may feel fairly reasonable to us. At those times our only clue will be our child's reaction, which may well be to tell us to back off. We might feel hurt or indignant, since we are only trying to help them, but our children have correctly intuited that our 'help' is coming from a place of fear and control rather than trust, and that we are attempting to take over their journey, which in truth we are. Here are a few things we might do to soothe our worries.

We turn learning moments into teaching moments

Our child asks us a simple question about the moon, Egyptians, turtles, or whatever happens to be on their mind. We feel relieved that they are engaging in something vaguely academic, and seize upon this moment enthusiastically as an opportunity to teach them. Rather than giving them the answer they need to then continue whatever journey of discovery they're on, we talk at them. We share everything we know about this topic until their eyes glaze over, or they start to fidget, or just run out of the room. If we're lucky, they escape before we have time to completely kill their interest.

> They would show a little spark of interest in something and I would pounce on it. Looking back I can see how that must have felt for them. I remember once G, who is interested in nature, talking about bees, so I got all enthusiastic and went running off to print out a picture of a bee so we could learn all the different parts of a bee's anatomy. G just looked at me and said, 'I don't want to learn the parts of a bee.' Now I've learned to get curious instead of jumping in with my own agenda. He was fascinated with how the bees worked together for the good of the hive, and he wanted to learn more in his own way from YouTube and other places. I couldn't see that, though, because I was too focused on what I thought was important." CLAIRE

We sneak learning in

We come up with crafty ways to make sure our children are learning. We suggest a fun activity, like a nature walk or baking, and then suck the fun right out of it by making them look at the structure of pine cones or insisting they read the recipe out loud and do all the measuring. Nature walks and baking are both brilliant ways to learn so many valuable things, but when we're forcing it, our child picks up on our worries, and we turn something enjoyable into a chore.

We get overly excited about their interests

Our child expresses an interest in judo, chemistry, game design or drawing birds, and within minutes we're researching courses, books, documentaries and local groups they could join. We are filled with excitement for the promise this interest holds. Perhaps we hope they will make some new friends through it or are relieved that they are finally doing something we think is worthwhile. We might even catch ourselves daydreaming about the future. Perhaps this interest has career potential to it. The only problem is that our child isn't seeing it as we are. They may just be exploring the idea (and some ideas are only for exploring – or just a little stepping stone to the next thing). And our enthusiasm is likely to just put them off.

> " Any sense that I was trying to manipulate them to get them to do something and they would back off completely. You can put them off things that they love by doing that. So now they laugh and tell me to chill out because I'm getting too enthusiastic and trying to take over. I don't think anyone likes to be told what to do. It's a human need to have autonomy and to feel that you've got some control over your life." **HAYLEY**

We encourage them to produce some output

We see they're learning about all sorts of things and we're delighted. They keep sharing nuggets of information and things they're finding interesting, and we're having all sorts of fascinating conversations. Now if they could just write out a few words about it, we'd have something to show other people to prove that this is working. I think about how I would feel if someone insisted that I wrote something about a topic I was learning about for no other reason than to provide proof that I really had learned it. I'd find that annoying too.

We judge their activities

There's a powerful hierarchy of children's activities reinforced over and over again. Somewhere at the top are all the worthy things, like reading, writing and maths. Also up there are playing a musical instrument, science experiments, strategic board games, and pretty much anything that involves 'fresh air'. Way down at the bottom, we have gaming and anything else to do with screens, often dismissed as a waste of time. This is extremely problematic when our children are self-directed. If we are judgy about their activities, we not only undermine our relationship, but it will be hard for them to be discerning in their choices or to feel trusted by us.

We get overly attached to the outcomes of what they do

It's absolutely natural for us to feel some attachment to what our children do. If they have interests that light them up or friendships that make them happy, of course we don't want these things to stop. But if you catch yourself in a state of panic when your child chooses to move on from an interest, a friendship or a group they've been part of, there's almost certainly some underlying fear. Are we holding on to things we perceive to be solutions? Why don't we trust their choice to move on to new interests and new friends?

We think more about what they do than how they are

We live in a very doing-focused society, and there is obviously nothing wrong with doing. But it's important to differentiate between the doing that comes from the feeling that we are expected to be busy, and the doing that naturally arises when we are connected to our internal navigation system that we talked about in Chapter 2. When our children are learning from home, we have the opportunity to help nurture that connection in them. If we are focusing solely on whether they are busy and whether they are doing things that we consider to be of value, we may well be missing out on how they are and what is driving them.

Catastrophic thoughts

Any of these things can move quickly from slight worry to catastrophic thinking. As our body chemistry shouts at us to take action, the thoughts spiral, and the sensations become even more uncomfortable. Our desire to immediately solve the issue grows, along with our tunnel vision.

Some catastrophic thoughts we may have include:

- They'll always be behind.
- They'll never get a job.
- They'll never have a group of friends.

- I'll never have a life of my own again.
- They'll never do any proper learning.

Whenever you catch yourself using the words 'never' and 'always', you know you are catastrophizing!

So what can we do?

Cultivating the observer

The first step towards change is becoming aware of when we have triggered an old pattern and, instead of reacting, seeing if we can pause and pay attention to it. For this, we need to introduce the observer into our lives – that part of us that recognizes when we're falling back into old patterns, gently taps us on the shoulder, and says, 'Hey, look, you're doing it again!' Once we manage to spot our reactivity, we have a much better chance of pausing before we spin off down an all-too-familiar and unhelpful pathway.

Imagine you feel anxious about your child not learning maths. You keep suggesting that they do some maths, and they keep telling you they don't want to. This makes you feel more anxious and the problem grows in your mind. You start to worry that they'll end up behind their former classmates, which leads you to think that they'll never catch up, and you wonder how they'll ever get a job if they never do maths. Then you feel concerned that maybe your child will never get a job and it will be entirely your fault. Each time the topic of maths comes up it feels even more tense and charged, your child becomes even more resistant, and your relationship starts to suffer. Tunnel vision has set in. All you can think about is solving the problem about maths, but your heightened reactivity stops you from considering new perspectives or learning more about your child. You just want to solve the problem!

In your head, of course, there's a simple solution – your child happily doing maths. And in your reactive state, that may be the only solution you have access to. The reality, though, is that from this present battleground, the only thing you're creating is more resistance and further strain on your relationship. So what is the solution? Well, there could be many ways forward, but before you are open to seeing any of them, you need to take a pause and recognize your discomfort. Your only way to get out of the cycle of resistance is to stop resisting and take a closer look.

By noticing the thoughts, feelings and sensations in the body that accompany the trigger, we'll find that we are able to bring in new perspectives and shift the course of our thoughts. From there, rather than our old knee-jerk reaction, we'll be able to choose the response that is in our and our children's best interests. In the following three chapters, we'll look at how we can open our mind to bring in kindness and curiosity about what's happening. For now, though, let's focus on the hardest part – simply noticing.

Noticing the 'feeling tone'

How do you feel when an old neural pathway lights up and you get triggered? Do you feel your heart rate soar? Do you want to scream? Can you feel your muscles tensing up? In the last chapter we talked about how our sympathetic nervous system pulls out all the stops to keep us safe. We don't just think about fighting or running away; we feel it in the body.

For example, when we interpret something in a way that makes us feel ashamed, as well as calling to mind similar experiences from the past and catastrophizing about the future, we may also feel the blood rush to our cheeks and a racing pulse. When we're angry, along with intense thoughts might come tense shoulders and a tight jaw.

You may experience any of the following physical reactions when your sympathetic nervous system is triggered:

- rapid breathing
- tight throat
- quickened pulse
- tense muscles
- clenched jaw
- tight chest
- knot in stomach
- sinking feeling.

There's a term in Sanskrit – *vedana* – which is sometimes translated as 'feeling tone'. This is a helpful way to think about all the ways in which we respond to life: our thoughts, feelings and physical sensations. Just recognizing the feeling tone of your triggered moments is a huge step towards a new way of living with your child.

> " I can tell when something is off as I'll feel it in my body, like a resistance. And then I'll immediately think no, then I take a moment and reflect on it. I have to take a few steps back. Sometimes I'll tell the children that I need a minute. I may have to come back and say sorry because I got something wrong. I try to really work out what's the worry here. Normally the worry is me thinking they'll do something forever, or that there's something that they'll never do. Normally I find that it's a silly worry." HOLLY

Staying with the trigger

Once we recognize the familiar feeling tone of the trigger, we can see if we have the capacity to stay with it rather than try to escape the discomfort. When we are fearful or anxious, our mind tends to jump between scouring the past for information to back up its hypothesis, and projecting doom and gloom into the future. Rather than attempt to change these thoughts when their momentum is at its highest, it is far easier to move our attention away from them. By choosing instead to move our awareness to the physical sensations of the trigger, we lessen the noise in our heads that is almost certainly busy piling on additional layers of fear and worry.

'Doing' mode and 'Being' mode

The terms 'Doing' and 'Being' are often used in mindfulness, and are helpful for understanding why the busy mind keeps us spinning in circles, and how staying present to the feelings and sensations of the present moment can be transformational in our lives.

Doing mode can be depleting

The Doing mode is our brain's way to be fast and efficient when something needs to be solved or ticked off a list. In Doing mode the mind looks at where we are and where we want to go, and then focuses on the gap between and the best way to close this gap. This is effective if you're preparing for a day out, getting some work done or arranging an activity. However, because it is all about getting things done, it is far less helpful when the problem is not a practicality to be solved but an uncomfortable emotion. Then, our Doing mind, convinced it needs to solve the problem, ruminates and worries, making things feel even worse and digging the hole deeper. If you've ever felt like you're drowning in a problem, you're almost certainly in Doing mode.

The Doing mode is greatly celebrated in our society and it is the default mode for most of us. In fact, it sometimes feels like most of us spend our lives attempting to close gaps. And when your child first comes out of school, it is hard not to see life as a series of gaps to close. If you are triggered, or life just seems resistant and difficult, you are almost certainly in Doing mode.

Shifting into Being mode

In Being mode, we are connected to our bodies and the present moment. The mind is not whirring away trying to fix things. It is not judging and assessing gaps and how to close them. Our senses are alive and we feel rooted in our experience. The present moment might well have its challenges, but in Being mode we don't feel rushed to solve anything or change any aspect of our experience. There is no gap to fill!

Because most of us are so used to living for the most part in the less conscious Doing mode, it requires practice to be able to make the shift into Being mode. We often rely on external things – a hug from our child, a beautiful sunset, a rare moment of calm or a piece of music – to pull us away from scattered thoughts and jolt us into the present moment. We can recognize when we come into Being mode because our senses come alive, the noise in our brain quietens and we feel in touch with a deeper part of ourselves. We see the nuances, the richness and the fullness of the moment. If things feel light, easy and generally flowing downstream, it is likely that we are in Being mode.

Mindfulness practices to help you find the pause button

When we practise mindfulness, we are practising shifting into Being. Many parents are put off mindfulness because they think it's insanely unrealistic, particularly if they are already stretched thin. So it can be helpful to imagine that Being mode is always there, often hidden underneath layers and layers of Doing. This is far less about achieving another state of mind than about letting go of the busy, always-achieving mind, and sinking down into that soothing place below all the noise and the worries.

The next time you feel triggered, try one of these simple practices to help you ground back into your body and away from spiralling thoughts. The more you do these practices, the quicker and easier it will become for you to press the pause button.

Take slow breaths

By slowing our breathing down, we send a message to the brain that the threat has passed, allowing the fight-or-flight response to subside. While rapid breathing is a sign that the sympathetic nervous system is switched on, slow breathing calms us by activating the parasympathetic nervous system. Additionally, slow, deep breaths can stimulate the release of endorphins, the body's natural feel-good chemicals. No matter where you are when you feel triggered, try simply slowing your breathing down, and notice how things shift.

The three-step breathing space

This practice provides an easy and accessible way to cultivate awareness of our feeling tone and bring a sense of calm and presence to a challenging moment:

1. *Become aware.* Adjust your posture so that you are sitting or standing straight. If possible, close your eyes. Notice what thoughts are going through your mind, what feelings you're aware of (anger, frustration…) and what sensations are present in your body (tightness, heaviness…).
2. *Focus on your breath.* Direct your attention to the physical sensations of the breath. Follow the breath, noticing the air against your nostrils as you inhale and exhale, the rise and fall of the chest and belly, the sinking of the shoulders. Use the breath to anchor yourself in the present moment. Take a few breaths here.
3. *Expand your attention.* Now expand your attention around your breath to include the body as a whole, including your posture and facial expression. As you breathe, imagine your whole body is breathing. Take a few breaths here. And now, open your eyes and notice any change in how you feel.

Finding your anchor

This is such a simple practice, but it is incredibly effective for escaping an over-busy mind and coming back into connection with your body. You can do the whole practice in a quiet space and with your eyes closed – it is a great way to become familiar with sinking into the body and shifting into Being. Then, when you need to call on the practice to find your ground in a difficult moment, you can hone in on the anchor that is most effective for you, keeping your eyes open if the situation requires:

1. *Close your eyes (if possible) and take a couple of slow breaths.* If you are triggered, notice how your body feels and how the trigger is playing out. Pay attention to the feeling tone of this moment. What thoughts, feelings and physical sensations are present right now?
2. *Move your attention to your feet* and spend a few minutes noticing how your feet feel – the pressure of the soles of the feet on the ground, the heels, the tops of the feet, the toes. Notice if you can feel your socks or shoes. Be aware of any sensations, such

as tingling, weightiness or sensations of hot or cold. Don't try to change anything; just observe how it all feels.

3. *Now move your attention to your hands* and apply the same curiosity. If your hands are touching each other, notice where they meet and what sensations are present. If they are resting in your lap, notice the pressure, or any sensations of hot or cold that are there. Become aware of the palms of your hands, the backs of your hands, your fingers and your thumbs, registering how they feel.

4. *Now move your attention to your breath.* Notice the cool air on your nostrils as you inhale, and the expansion of the chest and belly, and then follow the breath as you exhale, the chest and belly falling, and perhaps the shoulders also sinking. There may be one place that you feel the movement of the breath most, in which case you can also choose to just zone into this one place.

5. *Finally, go back to whichever anchor feels most effective for you right now*, and rest there for a few more moments. Then open your eyes. Notice how you feel now.

Ways to cultivate Being mode with your child

These two practices are a wonderful way to shift into Being and pay attention to your child in the present moment. Enjoy resting that busy Doing mind and simply seeing and appreciating your child, exactly as they are.

Create mindful moments with your child

Bring awareness to something you routinely do with your child. This could be playing a game, brushing their hair, helping them dress or reading, for example. Have no goal except to be aware and in the moment. Simply notice how it feels to pay attention to your child and to how you engage with them. If you find your mind shifting away, be kind to yourself and gently come back. If something comes up that you find irritating or distracting, see if, instead of allowing your thoughts to spiral, you can just notice it instead.

Observe your child

Choose five minutes this week to observe your child as unobtrusively as possible, perhaps when they're eating, playing or watching TV. Notice how they sit or lie, the texture of their skin, their hair, the clothes they're wearing, their breathing. Just observe them without assumptions or judgements. And again, if something pops up for you, just notice it instead of engaging with it.

Look for the 'Glimmers'

'Glimmers' is a term coined by Deb Dana, a leading expert in the field of Polyvagal Theory.[1] Unlike triggers, which activate the fight-or-flight response, Glimmers are micro-moments of safety and connection that help us feel calm and regulated. We could say that they are little doors into Being mode. They help us in many ways, by countering our natural negativity bias, regulating our nervous system and enhancing our mood with their accompanying dose of feel-good dopamine.

The key to catching Glimmers is to become attuned to noticing them. So, just as we cultivate awareness of our triggers and pause to notice the sensations, so we can cultivate awareness of Glimmers, spotting when there is a little positive moment for us to enjoy, and noticing how it makes us feel. A smile from a stranger, the sun on our face, the smell of a garden after the rain, a compliment from a friend. Don't rush on by! Sink into the present moment and savour the beauty of these little moments. The more you practise, the more Glimmers you'll see every day.

---

1   See www.rhythmofregulation.com

Journal prompts

- What day-to-day things do you find most triggering with your child? Take a look at the ones you have listed.

- How do you usually react in those moments? Is it helpful?

- How does your child normally respond to you?

Chapter summary

- To free ourselves from our fears and conditioning, we need to move beyond just understanding theories and dig deep into our patterns.

- Many things about learning out of school are likely to trigger old stories about ourselves.

- Typically, when we are triggered, we respond by trying to control things.

- By cultivating the observer, we can spot when we are triggered by learning to recognize the sensations.

- Using mindfulness-based tools we can find a pause when we're triggered, and avoid going down the old neural pathways

Chapter 9

Step 2: Be kind

As you start to notice your fears, you'll realize that deschooling involves challenging beliefs and patterns that you've lived with for many years. Taking a closer look at these inevitably means reconnecting with all sorts of vulnerable places that you might have spent decades ignoring or preferring not to think about. As your child keeps shining the light on these places, you may feel regret, anger or sadness about things in your life that you wish you'd handled differently, or about ways you've interacted with your child in the past. If your response to becoming aware of these patterns is to give yourself a hard time, you'll just keep digging those old grooves deeper, making the whole process of deschooling far harder. To move beyond habitual patterns and beliefs, and to choose new, more aligned ways to respond to life, we need to resist the urge to run away or negate them. Instead, we have to learn to be with them and to welcome their presence so that we can look at them more closely. How can we move in close to a challenging thought if we beat ourselves up or feel despair every time we think of it? It doesn't just take courage to step off the beaten track; it takes a lot of kindness too.

Now that we've paused, the most important qualities we can introduce to the space are self-compassion and curiosity. Self-compassion helps us calm down and feel safe, and curiosity helps us see a bigger perspective. So before we get curious about our child, first we need to tend to ourselves. Step 2 is 'Be kind.'

- Step 1: Pause!
- **Step 2: Be kind**
- Step 3: Be curious
- Step 4: Engage

Self-compassion

How self-compassionate are you?

Imagine a good friend is struggling in some way. Take a moment to picture yourself listening and responding to them. Imagine what you might say, the kind of words you'd choose, your tone of voice, your facial expression, and whether you might hug them or offer some kind of comforting touch. How would you try to help your friend feel?

And now imagine that it's you who's struggling, and think how you would treat yourself. What would you say to yourself? What words and tone would you use? How would you try to make yourself feel?

If you're like most people, you'll have found that you were far more gentle to your friend than you were to yourself. We often intuitively know what our friends need from us, and don't think twice about offering it. We listen carefully and let them know that they are appreciated. We name all the qualities we love in them, and remind them that they are so much more than this temporary struggle. We insist that they are not to blame and that this sort of thing happens all the time to people. We give them a hug to reassure them that they are not alone, and tell them we're always there for them. Perhaps we suggest something that will help them feel better – a treat or some action that would ease the pressure. Yes, we know exactly what our friends need.

Yet, when it comes to our own struggles, instead of reminding ourselves of all our great qualities, we tend to dredge up all the other times we struggled in the past, and add those to our emotional load.

We look at how hopeless it all seems, then compare our lot to other people's and feel worse because everyone else seems to be getting it all so right. We might tell ourselves that we deserve this, that we're always getting things wrong and that we need to do better. Most of us wouldn't have many friends left if we dared treat them like we treat ourselves.

> Self-compassion has been more of a recent journey and it has hugely improved my well-being. I didn't really understand it before. I actually Googled it. I realized that I have high expectations of myself and others, so I felt disappointed quite a lot. It's important to understand if your expectations of yourself are even achievable, or are you setting yourself up to fail? I would write up a huge to-do list and tell myself I'd get it all done today. I can come out of a negative space quite quickly now. I talk to myself in a kind way. It's been about just understanding that there's so much more to being a human, and really allowing me to support myself." CLAIRE

What is self-compassion?

I remember when I first came across the term 'self-compassion', many years after I had begun to practise mindful meditation. Three things struck me as I started to incorporate the practices into my days. First, that self-compassion felt like the missing piece in my life. Second, how odd it was that in all my years (and particularly those of being a mother) it had never occurred to me that being kind to myself was important. And third, if I wanted my children to grow up to be kind to themselves, I needed to start by setting a decent example.

In simple words, we could think of self-compassion as the practice of being a good friend to ourselves. The term was put on the map in 2013, when researcher Kristin Neff, who had been studying self-compassion for some years, gave a popular TED talk about her findings.[1] Neff's research revealed the positive impact self-compassion has on our mental and physical health, linking it to lower levels of anxiety, depression and

---

1   See https://self-compassion.org

stress, and to enhanced immune function. When we are self-critical, our brains interpret this as being under threat, and we activate our fight-or-flight-system. In the rare case that we need to take specific action to get to safety again, this is effective. However, since the threat is usually in our heads alone, the activation of the stress response generally makes us feel even more alarmed and worried. In comparison, when we engage in self-compassion, we activate our care system, which soothes us and calms us down, recognizing that we are not under threat at all.

In day-to-day life, this translates as acknowledging when things are difficult, and holding ourselves with kindness. It doesn't mean giving up on our goals or being less resilient in life. In fact, neuroscientific findings show that self-compassion is a valuable aspect of emotional and psychological resilience, and helps us deal far better with the inevitable ups and downs of life. So, although you may think you're justified in berating yourself for all the ways you could be doing better as a parent, what your child really needs is for you to be kind to yourself. To use the aeroplane analogy, in order to hold space for our children, we have to put our own oxygen masks on first.

Neff defines self-compassion as combining three key elements: mindfulness, common humanity and self-kindness. If you think back to the exercise on how you would accompany a struggling friend, notice how we intuitively embrace all these elements when we are comforting someone else.

Mindfulness

When it feels like things are falling apart, we easily find ourselves overidentifying with whatever is going on, becoming overwhelmed or catastrophizing the situation in our minds. Bringing awareness to difficult moments allows us to look at them and understand that our interpretation is not an absolute truth (even though it may feel like that). So, rather than feeling like we actually are a complete failure, the lens of mindfulness helps us appreciate that even though this doesn't feel so good right now, that is mostly due to our perception. And, because our perception shifts and changes so easily, this is a temporary feeling. In the words of the old mantra, 'This too shall pass.'

Common humanity
When life is not going how we would like it to, it can feel as though these things only ever happen to us. This sense of isolation can be particularly powerful if we're feeling shame or a sense of inadequacy. At those times, it's easy to assume that everyone else has it all figured out and is having an easy time of it. It is comforting to remember that we all go through difficult times – this is part of being human, and it's really not just us! In the context of having left a school community, this sense of isolation can be exacerbated by feeling like you are being judged harshly or are the odd one out, even if you left by choice. It may take you a while to build a new community, and in the meantime, self-compassion is definitely your best friend.

Self-kindness
Instead of harsh self-talk and criticism, self-kindness encourages us to have a nurturing and supportive attitude towards ourselves. This involves treating ourselves with warmth and understanding, especially during particularly difficult times, or when we think we are failing at something. For people who have a strong inner critic, this can be the hardest part of self-compassion practice. I have met many parents whose demanding inner critic spurred them on through academic success and great achievements in their careers, but they eventually found themselves exhausted by their own *modus operandi* and were determined not to pass it on to their child. To make the mammoth shift from harsh critic to best friend can be extremely challenging but, like everything in deschooling, this is an intentional practice, which will create big shifts over time.

Why are we so hard on ourselves?

Evolutionary wiring
In times gone by, self-criticism might have served the purpose of pointing out where we should take corrective action to keep ourselves safe. If flouting one of the rules of the tribe resulted in us feeling an

unpleasant emotion like shame, we'd be naturally encouraged to toe the line, and avoid getting kicked out. In the context of modern society, with so many expectations and confusing layers of complexity, this mechanism can end up feeling like a constant malfunctioning of the system. And not only does it make everything feel even worse, but it isn't actually helpful. It's far more likely to lead to denial, escape or paralysis than to meaningful action.

We're not a compassionate society
Alas, despite all the research into the benefits of self-compassion, it's hardly a core value in our society. From an early age, we are encouraged to be continually improving ourselves and comparing our achievements with others. The school system itself, based on gradings, comparison and striving for results, actively encourages self-criticism and a pervasive need to keep trying harder. A common thread throughout parenting is the sense of never being enough, no doubt fed by a toxic combination of lack of support coupled with internalized social expectations, from how many hours your baby sleeps, to the kind of food you prepare and whether they are reaching their milestones. These expectations might later morph into how many extra-curricular activities your child does, whether you all eat harmoniously around the dining table in the evening and how good your child's GCSE results are. There will always be something we should be doing better, and as parents, we can be our own harshest judges.

Why learning beyond school can make us hard on ourselves

There are several aspects of unschooling that can lead us to be particularly hard on ourselves:

- The lack of a model to follow makes us prone to self-criticism and worry that we're doing it all wrong.
- We may feel like other people are judging us.

- We might have less time for practices that nourish us (unless we prioritize them).
- We may lack like-minded people to encourage and believe in us.

But self-compassion is a key piece in our deschooling process:

- Deschooling is extremely challenging if we're not kind to ourselves. When we talk to ourselves harshly, we increase the triggered feelings and make everything worse by adding to our sense of discomfort.
- If we want our children to grow into self-compassionate adults, then that is what they need to see in us. We have to model self-compassion to our children.
- It's harder to be compassionate to our children if we're not compassionate with ourselves.

When the journey to deschooling is particularly stressful

Your inner critic is likely to be particularly harsh if you have previously navigated a difficult time in the school system. Parents who have taken their child out of school in challenging circumstances may find that rather than jumping into learning beyond school with enthusiasm, they are burned out from navigating school avoidance, anxiety and the consequences at home of their child's needs not being met. This may have all entailed endless meetings with schools and professionals, heaps of self-doubt about their parenting, and an enormous amount of worry about their child's mental health. The toll from this experience can be severe for parents and children, and it's common for parents to feel disempowered and with a strong inner dialogue around failing. They may also feel extremely alone now with the responsibility for their child's mental health. Added to the pressure can be the sense that people are scrutinizing their every move. This is fertile ground for harsh self-talk, which will not only make their own life stressful, but will also make it far harder to hold the space confidently for their child.

If this is your story, then bringing self-compassion to your life is an essential part of your journey beyond school. Every time you wonder if you are doing enough or if it is all enough, take a deep breath and come back to the self-compassion practices at the end of this chapter.

We must first be good parents to ourselves

Lots of advice for parents seems designed to make parenting as miserable as possible. A battle of wills, an exercise in discipline and consistency, a constant quest to get everything right and to make sure that everyone and everything turns out perfectly. However, this kind of advice generally misses out one huge detail, which is that, as the primary space-holder for our children, how we are and how we feel matters more than almost anything else. You'll almost certainly have noticed this in action. When your own cup is full and you feel generous towards yourself, your mood is likely to be spacious and appreciative. You'll be noticing all the lovely things that are happening that day and allowing yourself to relax in the 'enoughness' of it all, and of yourself. Your child picks up on this energy and feels a sense of safety and acceptance. You're not necessarily thinking about how you're interacting with them, but things just seem to flow in a good-natured way.

If, on the other hand, you wake up worried about the day, concerned about what your children are learning and doing, and giving yourself a hard time about all the things you're getting wrong, your presence doesn't feel so light. You don't notice all the good stuff, but you do notice all the details that are a bit off. Their choice for breakfast could have been healthier, they haven't read anything for a couple of days, there's a bit of tension between siblings, you think you should have planned a trip out but you haven't. All these things add to your panic and the internal critic's voice gets louder. You try to correct this by making some suggestions in a playful voice, but your face and voice show the tension and your child spots the confusing mismatch. Your jumpiness is making their nervous systems feel a little less safe and a little less relaxed. The space no longer feels conducive to all those things that help a child thrive – connection, acceptance, belonging and safety.

> " I was getting more and more on edge about the lack of things happening. My daughter was just getting on with the things she loves, but I could feel all the old school pressure on me, and all I could think was that this isn't enough and that I'm really failing at it all. She started getting on edge too, because I was so jumpy about everything. It finally came to a head when I started to insist that she did certain activities that she really didn't want to do and she started crying. She asked me why I think that what she does isn't enough. I realized I was just projecting my own sense of not being enough onto her." RHONDA

If we are forever striving to get things right, and criticizing ourselves for not getting there, we are unlikely to be holding a space in which our children feel truly relaxed and accepted. Do we have to always be in an upbeat and cheerful mood? No. Life happens, and there will be inevitable ups and downs that we will have to navigate. Should we value feeling good? Yes. Is it okay to replace trying to make it perfect with just feeling good with what we have? Yes, absolutely.

What happens when we are kind to ourselves

We have the capacity to hold more
When we are kind and forgiving to ourselves, we can be more compassionate and understanding of our children, because we no longer need them to fit a particular narrative of what successful parenting looks like to help us feel okay about ourselves. If we blame ourselves for every challenging moment, or are unforgiving of all the times that we get things wrong, we are more likely to need our children to toe the line for us. If we feel like we are failing at motherhood when our child has a tantrum, it becomes far harder to be with our child during the tantrum. Not only is our child having a hard time, but we're a failure. By accepting and being gentle with our own emotions, we are more able to accept and be gentle with our children's emotions. When we silence the inner critic, we can relax.

We model self-compassion to our children

If I am ever in need of guidance, I find it helpful to imagine how I would like my children to live their lives when they are my age, and I pretty much always find the answer right there. Would I like them to give themselves a hard time whenever they get something wrong, or to feel inadequate if something doesn't go their way? Definitely not. I'd like for them to be kind and accepting of themselves, and to not have a voice telling them they should have done better. And if that's what I would like for my children, then, to the best of my abilities, that is what I have to nurture in myself.

An incident some years ago comes to mind. I was with my daughter, who was about five at the time. I had forgotten to send an important email and was annoyed with myself. I shook my head and said out loud something along the lines of, 'I can't believe I'm so stupid.' I had a little pang of regret that I'd voiced it like that, but then forgot about it. A week or so later and we were sitting at the table together, both drawing pictures. My daughter wasn't happy with what she'd done and screwed it into a little ball. 'I can't believe I'm so stupid', she announced, as she threw it crossly onto the table. It was a wake-up call for me – not only that I shouldn't verbalize that kind of self-critical thought, but that it wasn't deserved it in the first place.

Whether we like it or not, our children are observing us. They can see when we are hard on ourselves and when we treat ourselves with kindness. If we want them to be gentle to themselves, then we can start right now to show them what that looks like.

> " Self-compassion is one of the things I'm definitely not very good at, and my children are pivotal in helping me to learn to be kind to myself. My self-talk is terrible and my children pick me up on it all the time. They say to me, 'Why do you talk to yourself like that? Because you don't want us to talk to ourselves like that, do you?' I have a lot of fear of judgement. I had a very traumatic childhood, so I think I have a deep sense of rejection. My eldest two will often reflect on things I do, and then they'll say, 'I think that comes back to your deep sense of rejection. We're not going to reject you, Mum.'" HAYLEY

Self-compassion practices

So how can we turn to self-compassion when we're feeling challenged? Once you've hit the pause button, and before you do anything else, first tend to yourself by using one of the following self-compassion practices.

Supportive touch

When our child is upset, we instinctively want to hug them. This is because we intuitively know that a caring touch activates the parasympathetic nervous system (also sometimes known as the care system). As the body releases oxytocin and breathing slows down, the fight-or-flight response calms down in the knowledge that the threat is over. When we hug our child, we help them feel safe. If we're lucky, we have a person or people in our lives who also do this for us. But, whether we do or we don't, we can always bring supportive touch to ourselves.

This is a soothing practice if you're feeling challenged or emotionally reactive. You can spend a few minutes on it, or discreetly introduce it into any difficult moment to calm your nervous system.

1. Take a couple of deep breaths.
2. Gently place your hand over your heart, noticing the changing sensations from the warmth of your hand, and the feeling of contact.
3. Hold your hand still or make small circles, applying a very gentle pressure. Notice how your chest rises and falls as you breathe in and out.

Here are some other options you can explore. For some people (including our children) touch can trigger sensory overwhelm. If that's the case for you, I suggest that you try the last option of just cupping one hand in the other, or see if you can adapt one of the other suggestions so that it feels comfortable for you:

- one hand on your cheek

- cradling your face in your hands
- gently stroking your arms
- crossing your arms and giving a gentle squeeze
- one hand on your abdomen
- cupping one hand in the other in your lap.

Self-compassion break

The self-compassion break consists of three phrases that evoke the three fundamental qualities of self-compassion: mindfulness, common humanity and self-kindness. You can introduce this into a pause to help you stay present with particularly strong emotions, or use it after a difficult time. You can incorporate the supportive touch as you do this practice – bringing your hand to rest on your heart, for example. Change the phrases to wording that deeply resonates with you:

> 'This is hard right now' (mindfulness), or 'This really hurts', 'This is very stressful.'

> 'Everyone suffers sometimes' (common humanity), or 'Other people feel this way too', 'Struggling is just part of being human.'

> 'May I be kind to myself' (self-kindness), or 'What do I need to hear right now to express kindness to myself?', 'What do I need right now?'

Self-compassion can be surprisingly challenging

Some people find self-compassion difficult, particularly if they grew up in an environment in which being kind to yourself might have been dismissed as a weakness. If it feels like that for you, then try simply asking 'What do I need right now?' You can also start with the soothing touch that feels the least intense – perhaps just cupping your hands together, for example.

Name the deeper pattern

If you recognize that whatever is going on with your children has triggered a deeper pattern of your own, it can be helpful to name it. 'Ah, this is that feeling of not-enoughness' or 'This is me feeling overwhelmed.' As you become expert at noticing how things feel in the body, you might notice that different thought patterns are accompanied by a different feeling tone. By being kind to yourself and naming the pattern, you'll find that not only does the pattern start to lose its sharp edges, but that you create space around it, and it becomes less overwhelming.

What do you need right now?

Perhaps, as you bring kindness to this moment, you realize that this is mostly about you and has little to do with your child. In which case, what do you need right now? What would shift your mood, support you or reassure you? Create a list of things that you can easily call upon in these moments – a chat with an understanding friend, a walk, listening to some music, or maybe just a big cuddle with your child.

> If I feel disappointed and grumpy about something, I might just find something of my own to get on with, so I'm not bringing my mood into her space. Or I might say that I'm feeling a bit grumpy and I need a walk. I can't sit and think my way out of it. If I'm depleted, I'm more likely to blame her in my mind for what's going on." RHONDA

> My strategy, personally, is to get outside. And if I can't actually get outside, to look out of the window. I actively look for a tree to just focus my eyes on and I breathe. But if I'm outside, I quite quickly reset with just having fresh air on my face. Nature restores me, and when things are really difficult, having a few emergency breathing techniques. Breathing and nature are my first aid." DONNA

My journey with self-compassion

Self-compassion did not come easily to me. I had, like many other mothers I know, tended to take full responsibility for just about everything that happened in the family, from the banal (no clean socks) to the emotional (someone feeling sad or hurt). I was a fixer, so I hung on to the idea that it was up to me, not just to ensure the smooth running of the whole operation, but also to make things better when they didn't go as planned. If everyone wasn't happy, I must be doing something wrong. My brain would go into overdrive, thinking of solutions, while also blaming myself for it ever happening in the first place. I should have done better. I should have said something else. I should have noticed something I didn't, etc., etc. This was a pattern that had also been a big part of my working life for over 20 years, and which led to my eventual burnout.

I initially felt a lot of resistance to the self-compassion practices because they challenged this long-standing version of me as an invincible person who had the power to fix things. There wasn't much room in there for being vulnerable and the practices felt quite alien. But, as I persevered, I started to find huge relief in this practice of being kind to myself, and many things that had felt immovable started to shift. When things didn't go to plan, just being there for myself took away much of the additional fear and worry my mind would create by berating myself. And I particularly noticed that my capacity to stay open and compassionate with my children, even in challenging moments, greatly increased. I began to understand that my needs were important too, and to make time for things that had no other purpose than to feel good – seeing friends, running, writing, taking a long walk even when no one else wanted to come. Keeping my cup full stopped feeling like a luxury or something to postpone for some future moment when there would be more time for me, and it began to feel like an essential part of my life.

Journal prompts

- How do you talk to yourself when things are difficult? Are you hard and judgy, or are you a good friend to yourself?

- How do you think the way you treat yourself affects how you hold space for your children?

- How do things shift when you do the self-compassion practices?

Chapter summary

- Self-compassion is essential for deschooling because it inevitably involves looking at old stories about ourselves and can take us to some vulnerable places. If we're hard on ourselves, it becomes harder to do this work.

- We tend to be far harsher judges of ourselves than we are of other people. Self-compassion is all about learning to be a good friend to ourselves. By doing so, we calm our nervous system and create space for understanding and growth.

- We live in a society that does not encourage self-compassion, and if the path to leaving school was stressful for your family, you may be particularly harsh on yourself.

- Cultivating self-compassion not only fosters emotional resilience but also enhances our ability to respond to life's challenges in more constructive ways.

- By practising self-kindness and understanding, we create a nurturing environment where our children learn to be compassionate towards themselves and others.

Chapter 10

Step 3: Be curious

Congratulations! You've brought awareness to a challenging moment and pressed the pause button, intentionally stopping any old automatic reaction in its tracks. By tending first to yourself, your nervous system will feel calmer, and your capacity to take in new information and other perspectives increases. This is a huge piece of work and it sets you well on your path to accompanying your child in a way that feels more satisfying and joyful to both of you. From here, you have the ability to stop and survey the moment, lift up the veil of old beliefs and paradigms, and shine a light on what is really going on beneath. With our next step, you're going to bring a lens of curiosity to whatever may be going on. This is 'Step 3: Be curious.'

- Step 1: Pause!
- Step 2: Be kind
- **Step 3: Be curious**
- Step 4: Engage

What do we mean by being curious? In Chapter 8, you had the chance to zoom in on all the things you find particularly challenging about living and learning out of school. You probably noticed how many 'shoulds' play out in your mind every day. From what a good parent should do, to what learning should look like, to what your child should be engaging in. Getting curious means leaving these 'shoulds' behind and exploring the present moment. It means seeing what's actually there, rather than comparing it to any idealized version of life or ourselves we hold in our minds. In the next chapter, we'll look at how choosing to view life through this new, open lens will entirely shift the way we engage with life and with our children. But for now, let's just enjoy getting curious.

Discovering your child

A truly wonderful aspect of unschooling is that in the absence of trying to direct or lead your child, you get to discover who your child is. Real discovery is only possible when we observe our children through this calm, open and non-judgmental lens. Here, we can intentionally see and embrace them for their whole, unique selves. So, feel excited about this part of your journey. You're going to be deep diving into who this other human being is, what makes them tick, how they learn, what is meaningful to them, and all the ways in which they are different from you.

Prepare to be surprised!
For many parents, this part of the journey is both fascinating and transformative, and filled with huge lightbulb moments. If, until now, you have been following a more mainstream path, the 'shoulds' have likely been eclipsing the real richness of everyday life. Now, as you pay attention, you'll notice how powerful those old beliefs and conditioning are. My beliefs included (among other things) that maths must look like hard work, that gaming was bad, that boredom was to be avoided at all costs, and that there is no value in giving things up. On my personal list of 'shoulds' were all sorts of unrealistic ideas about myself as a mother, from how creative I should be, to the kind of food I should be preparing and the kind of community I should create.

Unpicking these beliefs and assumptions meant calming a sense of rising panic multiple times a day, while reminding myself to get curious. What are they getting from this YouTube channel? Why doesn't my daughter want to go back to an activity she seemed to like last week? What if I just don't feel creative today? As I leaned into these questions, I began to see so much that had just not been visible to me before. In many ways, I was really seeing my children clearly for the first time. Every day, I learned more about them, what excited and motivated them, how they learned, what was important to each of them, and their different natural rhythms. And as I learned more about them, I also learned an awful lot about myself.

Be humble

Until we embark on this journey, we tend to assume we know a lot more than we actually do about our children. Modern parenting norms don't leave much space for pondering and learning, or indeed for admitting we don't know it all. But a big part of our work now is understanding that our children know more about themselves than we can ever know. To know how to hold them in their living and learning, we need to fully recognize that we have a lot to learn from them and about them.

Four things that can sabotage our curiosity

1. Holding on to being right

Most of us are attached to being right. Whether in our relationships, our politics or our work, it gives us immense satisfaction to prove our point or to have the last word. But people rarely learn from each other when they are entrenched in their own viewpoint. As long as being right or proving our point is more important to us than partnering with our child, we will be stuck in the same old place with all the same old conditioning. To really be curious, we have to accept and acknowledge that our child's perspective is just as valuable as ours.

2. Leaping to the future

Our thoughts around our children are often clouded by our fears of the future. When we invite curiosity in, we are inviting it to the present moment, just as things are right now. Try not to make mental leaps into the future. It's natural to want to do this, as it may well soothe any discomfort you're feeling, but it will also cloud your vision and stop you from meeting your child where they are right now.

3. Fixating on the outcome

It is our cultural norm to be outcome-obsessed when it comes to parenting, but just like taking leaps into the future, fixating on the outcome stops us from seeing what's happening now. We talked in Chapter 2 about how unschooling and self-directed learning are about process, not outcome. In fact, as you practise Step 3, you might want to tape those words to your fridge – 'Process, Not Outcome!'

4. Our own stories

It can be quite a shock when you realize that a lot of things that trigger you about your child are about yourself and how you are perceived. We can feel very judged as parents, so when our children don't behave like we think other people would expect, it's easy to feel shame or embarrassment. But needing our children to be a certain way to make us more comfortable, although perfectly understandable, does little to support our relationship with them or their unique sense of self.

Turn to your child for the answers

It seems paradoxical, but in those moments when we are challenged by what our child is doing or saying, or by a thought related to our child, our parenting or to ourselves, observing our child is usually the best thing we can do. Often, the information we need is right there in front of us. So ask yourself, what can you see if you bring an observant lens to the situation? Here are some questions you can ask yourself as you cast your curious eye over things.

Do I know what my child is doing? Or am I making an assumption?

We can easily jump to conclusions about what our children are doing. Not so long ago, I went out to a community meeting, leaving my daughter playing a game she enjoys on her tablet, and in which she has a close group of friends that run a club together. I came back some time later, tired from long conversations about membership rules and obligations, and slightly irritated that we hadn't quite managed to nail things down in the meeting. I saw that my daughter was still on this game and assumed she was playing in the way she usually plays. Some more time passed until she came into the kitchen, laid her tablet down and told me that she was pretty tired. It turned out that over the previous few days she hadn't been playing, because she'd been working with friends in the game to sort out the membership rules of their club. Among many things, this small group of 12- to 14-year-olds had defined entry rules, uniforms, obligations, communication channels and how to terminate a membership if a member didn't play by the rules. They had divided this work between them all, agreed on it, and written it up so that it was available to all the members. Her group had made a lot more progress than my group had. I recognized that after all these years I still make assumptions, and I still sometimes forget how capable children are. Not only that, but it was a reminder that they are always moving seamlessly back and forth from what someone outside might call 'fun' to 'learning'.

Why is this activity meaningful to them?

Many parents find themselves exasperated by their children spending a lot of time watching videos that appear to have no valuable content, or playing online games that seem to require little skill. It can be perplexing that this is the choice their child is making, and the knee-jerk reaction is to express their disapproval and overtly or covertly ask the child to stop. Here in Step 3, however, we can be curious about the reason they've chosen this activity. We may not love the activity, but we can certainly try to understand our child. At plain sight, it may look like a waste of time, but what else might be there?

Perhaps there is a social aspect that our child needs or finds fulfilling. Maybe it's their chosen form of downtime, a way to relax before they do something else. There may be some aspect of what they're watching that fascinates them. Perhaps it has to do with older children, or some facet of life that they're curious about. If it's a game, perhaps they are enjoying becoming really skilled at something. Remember 'competence' from Self-Determination Theory in Chapter 2? Mastering a simple video game may be giving our child confidence. Or are they finding life stressful and using this activity as a refuge, as a safe place to be, a place where they can be in control? Perhaps the light-heartedness of it is helping them through something they're struggling with. If previously they had more restrictions, are they simply enjoying exercising their autonomy? And, of course, it could simply be that our child is bored and using this activity as a filler until they feel more inspired.

Once we lose the 'this is a waste of time' mindset, we can see that although the activity itself doesn't appear meaningful to us, there are many potential reasons why it has meaning for our child. And once we have a deeper sense of this, we can respond better to our child.

To really appreciate what your child is getting out of something, sit with them, take an interest, have a go at a game yourself. Look at it from their perspective, and see what you discover.

> Charlie is more like me so I probably find it easier to see the value in what he's doing. Because Max is interested in different things, it can be harder for me to see the value. I try not to judge, and it helps me to get onto his level and immerse myself in what he's doing. I find some things quite boring, so I have to not be negative, but if I don't necessarily want to do something, I still make sure he knows I value it." EVA

Do I have strong preconceived ideas about the activity?

Get curious about which activities make your heart sing and which put your teeth on edge. And watch out for that social hierarchy of children's activities – are you celebrating maths and scowling at video games? These prejudices can be extremely limiting as they lead us to glorify some things and underestimate others. The reality of how your child interacts with all these things is likely to be far more complex and nuanced. I've seen my children work extremely hard at a game and I've seen them have fun with maths, science and other 'academic' subjects. When one of my sons was about 12 he came into the kitchen looking quite stressed. It turned out that he was on a quest in a game that was really challenging. He was a bit fed up with it, but determined to get to the next level, so was going to have a break and then go back to it. To relax in the kitchen, he got out his German book and practised German for 20 minutes, and then, with a deep breath, headed back to the game. I was fascinated. The game was stressful and German was relaxing. Who'd have thought it?

> My kids' interests haven't been curriculum-based. When they love Minecraft or OMG dolls it can be hard to go, okay so what's the value in this? What shifted it for me is realizing that anybody can learn facts at any point in their lives, but what the kids are doing now is learning how they learn. So my son knows that if he wants to find things out, this is how he does it best, this is how he processes it. It's all about the process." HOLLY

Is this one of those process-not-outcome moments?

Personally, understanding this difference has been the most profound part of my deschooling. A child who can create their own learning journey will do so in a way that is coherent with who they are and where they are in the moment. They will inevitably make some choices that are aligned with them, but that seem odd to you. They may deep dive into something, and then leave it completely. They may stop going to an activity because it no longer interests them (even though you think it's wonderful). They may not want to engage in something you think would be great. Your child is becoming an expert at moving through life in a way that always feels right and coherent. Just as you certainly feel strongly about the way your life unfolds, so your child cares about theirs.

Meet them where they are in this journey by being curious about all the little choices they make. You'll soon find yourself no longer worrying about whether they made a 'good' or 'bad' choice, but seeing instead that each choice and decision is an important part of this process of always figuring out the next step. Enjoy watching the process unfold and bringing curiosity to how they make their choices. As you'll find in Chapter 11, this will make you a far more valuable ally for your child as they move through life.

> If they didn't do an activity in the way I thought it should be done, everything felt not good enough, so I was constantly disappointed in them and in me. At one point we did this visioning exercise so I could help them identify their passions and interests. S just stuck a picture of a football and some chocolate besides his name. I remember feeling disappointment and thinking that football can't be a vision. I told him that it wasn't enough, and I felt like we'd done it all wrong. I thought about the exercise recently. Now, he's 16 and his life is football, and that hasn't changed since he was 11. He's doing GCSEs now so that he can go to college to do football coaching; he reads about football, he plays football, he makes friends through football, and I can absolutely see that football is a part of his future. I look back and think, wow, I didn't trust the things that they knew, but now I do. It's a life plan and it's a valid life plan." CLAIRE

Am I being coercive? Do I have my own agenda?

How often do we get triggered because we have our own agenda and our children aren't playing along? It can be strangely hard to spot coercion, simply because it is such an acceptable part of modern parenting. There are endless books about how to get your child to behave how you want them to, and it can seem almost right that our children will naturally bend to our will simply because we are adults. But getting our own way just because we say so doesn't encourage our children to live fully into who they are. It is disempowering. So sometimes we may need to ask ourselves if our child may be simply reacting to our benign (to us, at least) tyranny.

This reminds me of a conversation I had with a parent who shared their frustration about a day out not going to plan with their three children, who were five, six and eight. The whole day seemed to be an exercise in the parent cajoling and insisting, with their children seemingly intent on resisting their every move. As they reflected on the day, they could see that they had had a fixed idea of what a fun day would look like and needed their children to go along with it. They realized that if they had taken some time to slow down and listen, and then work things out together, it would probably have gone much better.

Is my child advocating for themself?

What may look, through the lens of traditional parenting norms, like a child being 'difficult' may well be a child standing up for themselves. Perhaps they are in a social situation that feels uncomfortable, or they feel like they need more autonomy. If you're surprised by your child's reaction to something, see if you can delve a little deeper. Communication is hard, and we often need to look beyond the words to understand what need is being expressed.

> S is doing GCSEs and it's been interesting. It's so easy to get back into the mindset of planning and worrying about what they're doing, and I've found it a tricky time. I'm back to my fears again. So if I get wobbly and worry if he's on track, then I might approach him in a way that makes him ask me to back off. He'll say to me now, 'Mum, that's your worries, not mine.' He has the autonomy to be able to push back and call me out. Someone else might think it was disrespectful, but I love the fact that they call me out because they're right. I might find it uncomfortable in the moment, but actually, that's where my growth is." CLAIRE

How is my child right now? Are they happy?

There can be a natural tendency to look at what our children are doing rather than how they are. It's important to remind ourselves that the doing tends to come naturally when a child is happy and relaxed. If your child is doing something that is fun and relaxing, they are also in the perfect zone for acquiring new skills and learning new things.

If the question, 'Why are they making this choice?' has left you flummoxed, then ask yourself, 'Are they happy?' Is the sole purpose of this activity to be enjoyable to them? If that feels uncomfortable, have a think why that may be. Perhaps you might get curious about yourself and whether it feels okay for you to relax and have fun.

What do I need for myself right now?

We are far more likely to get triggered when we are overstretched or tired. At those times, it's normal for us to feel irritable when others don't go along with what we need, or to be sensitive to how we are perceived. But this lays a great responsibility on our children, and also means that you are unlikely to get what you need. As you bring curiosity to the moment, ask yourself what would help you right now – support, sleep, a friend to chat to, some activity of your own? In Part 3 of the book you're going to be deep diving into your own life and what you can put into place to support yourself and how you can set healthy boundaries for yourself.

> " My daughter teaches me so much about myself and our relationship and I find that really exciting because I am constantly having to question myself and sit in a non-judgmental place, which is quite hard and is massive growth for me. What I do is I go into a panic, then I make loads of lists of things I could do, and then I take a step back and say, 'Oh, I'm doing that again', and I look at the long lists of resources and courses, then I look at her and see that she's really happy. And ultimately, all I want is for her to be happy. Sometimes going for a walk, then coming back with a fresh perspective on it all." NICOLA

> " My ability to hold it all and be aware of my conditioning depends very much on how I am and what's going on in my life. I'm good at being aware, but it doesn't necessarily stop the emotion coming. Dialogue with other people and perspective help me be able to breathe through the difficult moments. Sleep, dialogue, meditation and yoga all help." EVA

Is it okay not to understand?

Yes! Sitting with the not knowing is a huge part of this. There can often be such a maelstrom of emotions and thoughts that it's hard to unpick it all. We won't always understand our children and we won't always know what to do, just as our partners and friends won't always understand us or know what to do. We're all complex human beings after all. In these times, give yourself a hearty dose of self-compassion and just try to stay in the moment with an open heart and an open mind. There is always something to be learned. Some of my most valuable lessons came out of moments when everything felt nebulous, only for the clouds to clear sometime later.

These are just some of the questions I have found useful over time. I encourage you to pause and reflect on whether there are any other questions you think would be helpful.

Staying present and connected

As we extend our curiosity to the moment and the people around us, it's easy to lose our ground and find ourselves triggered once more by a new thought or by something said to us. At this point, we can find that the calm pause we had created for ourselves all but disappears. You've probably noticed that it's far easier to calm your nervous system when you're by yourself, taking a walk in the woods, sitting on a yoga mat or just alone with a cup of tea. It is considerably harder to stay in the zone when we bring our children (or anyone else) into the mix. 50/50 awareness is a wonderful way to help you stay present and connected to yourself, while being curious about your child and the situation. You can practise this technique any time so you'll have it on hand when you really need it. Here is how you do it.

50/50 awareness

1. *Close your eyes (if possible) and zoom in on the sensations in your body.* Use the breathing and anchoring techniques from

Chapter 8 to connect with your body. Notice the sensations of your feet on the floor, your hands in your lap or the movements of your breath. Find the anchor that feels most grounding for you. Stay here for a few breaths.

2. *Open your eyes and notice what happens as you extend your awareness* to the environment around you, or as you interact with your child. Do you notice your attention leaving your body? Do you notice the mind kick into action as it thinks about what to say or starts to judge the situation? Practise holding your focus on the sensations in the body while still being aware of what's around you.

3. *If you are drawn away from your anchor*, just gently come back to it as soon as you notice.

When to nudge and when to hold back

Even with years of practice, it can be tricky to know when it's right for us to nudge something along and when it's right for us to hold back. For example, if there's an activity that you are absolutely sure your child would enjoy, but they say they don't want to go, do you just let it go, or do you try to convince them otherwise?

Unfortunately, there is no easy answer to this. The better you know and understand your child, and the more trusting your relationship, the easier it will be for you to discern what is most helpful, and for you to nudge a little when that feels right.

Lianne describes how this works with her daughter:

> "It's a fine line to know when to nudge and when to hold back. Her tendency would be to withdraw and get into a bit of a rut, so I've stepped in a few times and said that I really want her to try something. Sometimes it's worked and she's been really glad she did it, and other times she's said she doesn't want to do it again."

Jayne also stresses the nuances of this and how relationship-based it is:

> When you know your children, and you know the things that they find more challenging, find ways to support them in that, like pushing them a little bit beyond where they're comfortable but not too far, and just being there alongside them."

Perhaps the best thing we can do to help us know when to nudge is to ask ourselves a few questions:

Do I genuinely think that my child would enjoy this, or do I want them to do it to calm my own anxieties? Make sure you're clear on where your motivation is coming from. Are you sure this is something that your child would enjoy, or are you wishing they would enjoy it? They may well be saying no because it simply doesn't appeal to them. And if it's more about soothing your worries, your child might be picking up on unspoken expectations.

Is there some fear or anxiety that is preventing my child from doing the activity? If you think they may be saying no because the activity feels overwhelming in some way, see if there are ways you could support them. For example, they could try it but leave if they don't like it, or you could stay with them until you're both sure it's a good fit. Perhaps there's some more information that could be helpful. Ask them if there's something that would reassure them. Could you go early and meet the person in charge of the activity or check the place out first, for example? For some time, one of my children would only go to things that had a maximum of six children, so I would always call and check first. Eventually, they became confident enough that the size of the group was no longer an issue for them.

Do I know something they don't know? I realize that as I used to reel off things that sounded fun for us to do, my children didn't necessarily picture those things in the way that I did. What happens at forest school? How is an interactive workshop different from school? Try exploring ideas together so they can figure out what else they need to know in order to make a decision. It may be that as you look things up, new ideas emerge for other things they'd prefer to do.

Can I lessen the demand? If you are absolutely convinced your child would love the activity if they would just give it a chance, maybe you could have a lighthearted negotiation – for example, that they give it at least 20 minutes and then you both do something that they choose. Only do this if there isn't any deeper anxiety around the activity, and if you genuinely have no expectations of your child.

Am I pushing rather than nudging? If your child is telling you clearly that they don't want to do something, but you are pushing on regardless, you're likely to both end up cross and frustrated. There will be many, many other opportunities, so let them know it's okay and let go.

Some things will pan out and others won't, so never show disappointment or allow there to be any sense of failure when you nudge your child to do something and it doesn't work out. The more lightly you hold things and the more good-natured you are about it all, the more likely they will feel inclined to give things a go.

Journal prompts

- Write down the things you notice about your child when you start to get curious.

- What old stories of your own are showing up?

- How are these stories affecting how you see your child and what your child does?

Chapter summary

- Being curious takes us beyond our conditioning and assumptions and allows us to bring new perspectives to the present moment.

- We need to be intentional about being curious as our mind will easily sabotage our practice by trying to take us back to old patterns.

- Observing our child and asking ourselves questions about what they are doing and about their experience can often give us all the answers we need.

- Often, when we get curious about our child, we will realize that this is all about our own old stories, and really has little to do with them.

- Cultivating the ability to stay grounded in our own experience while also being curious is essential for ensuring that we don't unwittingly fall back into an old pattern.

Chapter 11

Step 4: Engage

Now that we have paused, given ourselves a big hug, become curious about our old stories and taken a closer look at our child, hopefully we feel calmer and are armed with new perspectives to figure out what comes next. We'll probably have seen that whatever we're feeling has as much to do with our own patterns and fears as it does with our child. And now that we've stopped an old pattern in its tracks, we have the headspace we need to respond to all the little nuances and complexities at play in the best way we can. Do we need to talk something through? Take a little break for ourselves? Or maybe just reconnect? The response we choose in this space won't come from fear, but from compassion, connection and curiosity.

For our child, this is also a fundamentally different space. Without our old stories running on autopilot, we are no longer hemming them into limited responses of their own. As we show our children that we are able to experience difficult emotions and still exercise the freedom to make intentional choices, we are giving them the space and the invitation to do the same. Welcome to 'Step 4: Engage.'

- Step 1: Pause!
- Step 2: Be kind
- Step 3: Be curious
- **Step 4: Engage**

A new space

A parent once told me about a challenging moment with their child. They had felt exasperated because their child refused to go to an activity that they usually enjoyed. The parent was surprised by how angry and frustrated they felt, but was able to find the 'pause'. They used their feet to anchor themselves in their body and to disengage from their spiralling self-talk, and did a discreet hand-on-arm self-compassion practice with the simple phrase in their head, 'This is really, really hard right now.' In the midst of the conflict with their child, they felt their body soften a little, and realized that they were tired and had been looking forward to a quiet hour to themselves while their child did the class. They also recognized that their child taking part in activities helped them feel better when their (rather sceptical) friends asked what they'd done all week. Their child refusing to go was triggering familiar feelings of unworthiness.

With all these realizations, their frustration with their child subsided and they no longer felt angry. They could see now that their child had their reasons that they as a parent didn't yet understand, and that their own reaction was as much to do with themselves as it was to do with their child: 'I still didn't really know what to do and my child was really upset with me because I'd been insisting. But it didn't feel like an urgent problem to solve any more. I just felt like I wanted to understand and to work it out with them.' They realized that they needed to reconnect before anything could shift. They apologized for getting annoyed and told their child it was fine not to go. Then they let the topic drop and suggested they both had a hot drink. The parent went on to recount:

> As the mood shifted and my child saw that I had lightened up, they told me that they didn't want to go to that class anymore but were a bit stressed as it felt like leaving would be letting the group down. Then they told me about the other things they wanted to do instead. We had a really good conversation about how it can be hard to move on from things and agreed that I would help then navigate this. We had

a hug and I feel like we both came out of it a little wiser and definitely on the same team.

As you move through the steps from 'Step 1: Pause!' to 'Step 4: Engage', you are likely to notice what this parent noticed – even when there is still some tension or worry, this space feels different. It's quieter, more open and less pressured. It is no longer a problem to be solved. To use the journey analogy again, when we are triggered, we zoom off down a familiar and well-worn highway in chase of a quick solution (even when it never really solves anything). We simply don't have the bandwidth for anything else. But when we soothe our nervous system, widen our perception and bring ourselves to a slow halt, we see that there are many other directions we can take. We know that we can't necessarily control the outcome but we can control which direction we choose. And when we are intentional about the direction, the outcome naturally tends to be better.

You'll know when you've reached this new space because it has the following qualities.

Relationship-centred

When we are triggered, our reactions can undermine our relationship with our children. Now that we no longer feel under threat, our focus is not on being right, proving ourselves or making sure things go our way. We don't need our child to act in a specific way or do a specific thing just to soothe us, and we don't need to resort to coercion to force an outcome. The lack of power-over dynamics reassures our child that they are heard and respected, and that their voice is as valid as ours. We naturally feel more compassionate and our focus returns once more to our relationship and on finding a solution that values everyone.

Open to possibility

It's scary to venture into the unknown, but this is where possibility lies. When you are anchored in the present moment and no longer hostage to old pathways, there are no foregone conclusions. Now that you are not catastrophizing or projecting into the future, there is no sense of 'here we go again' or that history is about to repeat itself, whether you like it or not. You may be surprised to find that even though you have no idea of how it will all turn out, you actually feel okay with that.

Safe

The feeling of safety this new space offers will be felt deeply by our children. When we are calm, steady and compassionate, our children know that they can express their feelings and opinions without fear of being shamed or dismissed, and without hurting our feelings or triggering us. And they have no doubt that we are on their side.

Present

As you no longer follow your brain down rabbit holes of the past or into an imaginary and calamitous future, you are likely to notice how much calmer and lighter life feels in the present moment.

Optimistic

When we understand that everything is a process, there is no despair or hopelessness. Even when things feel difficult to navigate, you'll be aware that there is an intrinsic value to it all, and that these moments, when moved through intentionally, always lead to somewhere a little more fulfilling.

Timeless

Everything feels urgent when we're triggered, but as we come back to a calmer place, the sense of urgency subsides. Your brain is no longer shouting that something desperately needs to be solved. You may still need to take action in some way, but you'll find that it's often fine to stop, breathe and take time to consider things before responding.

Empowered

In Chapter 2, we talked about what it means to be our whole selves. I think what surprised me most when I started to feel into this new space was how liberating it felt. When you get beyond all the noise of how things 'should' be, and all the old stories about yourself and fears about the future, you connect with a deeper intuition and a deeper confidence.

Vulnerable

It may seem odd that we could be both empowered and vulnerable at the same time, but perhaps that is one of the greatest things we learn on this journey. Showing up as our full selves means bringing everything along, including our vulnerabilities. In this new space, we're not pretending we know answers we don't know, we're not pretending to have all the solutions, or that we have any kind of power over our children that we don't have.

As we shift, our children shift too

Although our intention when doing this work should never be to change our children, what we will find as we keep responding from this space is that things will naturally shift. Look at any conflict that often arises in your home, and notice how things often play out to exactly the same script. When our nervous system is on edge, we will almost certainly elicit a reaction from our children that matches it. When we are calm, open and curious, we invite our child to also be calm, open and curious – we are no longer two nervous systems bouncing off each other. As we shift in the way we engage with our children, we give them more room to explore what's alive for them without being tangled up in all our stuff or rushed to figure things out quickly.

In the space that the aforementioned parent created, their child was able to consider and verbalize what they were feeling about the activity. If the parent had insisted that her child went to the class, she might have felt some temporary relief, but they would have both missed that moment of mutual trust and growth. Her child might have felt resentful or internalized the idea that giving things up is bad, no matter how you feel. Giving our children the space to work things through helps them avoid creating patterns that in the long term won't serve them well. Not only does this mean that we are able to navigate life together in a more fulfilling way; it also means that we model early on to our children that no matter what is going on around them, they can always choose how they respond and engage.

The communication dance

As we explore how we might respond to different situations, we should remember that communication isn't easy, particularly after a tense moment. Rather than believing that, as parents, we need to know exactly what to say or do and then stick to our guns, we might imagine it as an intricate dance, to be taken one step at a time. We may say or do things that completely miss the mark and accidentally provoke a reaction from our child. We may move away when our child wants us to come close, and we might try to connect when our child needs time for themselves. We may even find that as we talk things through we start to get triggered all over again. All we can do is stay aware of what is happening, look for the best next step and correct any missteps as we go.

What might your best next step be?
Get reconnected
Attempting to push through resistance or resentment will almost certainly lead to more resistance and resentment. If there has been tension, don't try to solve anything or talk things through until it's established that you're on your child's side and until they are also feeling calmer and more open to talking. If you feel like you've reached an impasse and don't know how to move beyond it, try letting go of whatever is causing the conflict and reaching for connection instead. Let your child see that although this is a tricky moment, you are valuing the relationship above everything else, and that you are confident that you'll figure it out together.

Say sorry and explain what's going on for you

If you realize that your old stories were driving you to act in a way that felt hurtful or unfair to your child, it's fine to recognize that and to say sorry. Sometimes, we inevitably get things wrong, and modelling our ability to see that and apologize is a great example for our children. If it feels appropriate and helpful, you could explain why you felt so challenged.

Choose fun over obligation

If curiosity leads you to realize that you are straining under all the weight of responsibilities and obligations, how about you just cut yourself some slack? Rather than your children be on the receiving end of your heavy conscience, enrol them in your quest for lightness. Put the radio on and dance. Put your wellies on and go for a walk in the rain. Have an ice cream. Play on the Wii together. Grab your list of 'Fun and connection' activities (see the end of this chapter), and have some guilt-free fun.

Help your child reconnect

Your conclusion in this space may be that your child needs some help to reconnect with their own motor. Just as we can learn to tap into things that reconnect us – some deep breaths in the garden, a walk or some music – so we can encourage our children to know and reach for what connects them to themselves. Cuddling a dog, playing with some LEGO®, running in the garden, getting cosy in an armchair – what might help them reset their nervous system? Nurture this ability in them, both by modelling it yourself and by making some gentle suggestions to them.

Shift the environment

Sometimes things may just feel a bit stagnant. Maybe the weather is grey and no one feels particularly inspired. Or perhaps an earlier disagreement is still lingering in the air. Rather than try to cajole unwilling people into doing something, see if you can shift the environment a little. Put on some music, open the windows, light a candle, make everyone a snack. Sometimes just a small shift in the environment can trigger bigger shifts in the general mood.

Consider if bigger shifts are needed

Maybe something does need to shift a little more. If you're going through a period where things don't seem to flow like they used to, then perhaps there are some bigger adjustments to make. You'll recognize when this is the case because the space doesn't feel quite so healthy, creative or connected as it maybe once did. Recognize that this isn't a sign of failure, but simply the way of things. As our children grow, their needs naturally change, and we'll sometimes need to stop and take stock of what's on offer and what else they need. Perhaps it's time for more trips out of the house, for investing time and energy in a new project or seeking out more activities and friendships in the wider community. Or perhaps the reverse is true, and it's time to relax and take things easier for a while.

Do nothing!

Many of our deschooling triggers will be all about us, and our children may be thankfully oblivious to our rising inner panic. In Chapter 7 we talked about how we react to thoughts as though they were real, and how easily one doubtful thought can catapult us into a spiral of negative self-talk. We might be triggered by something our child does or says. Perhaps they just announced that they hate reading, or they're looking a bit aimless. Or we may be thinking about a negative comment by a friend or family member. Where in the past our natural response to these situations might have been to panic and then either try to push our children to do something, or just sink into a pit of despair, we now have the resources to hold back and do nothing. Put all your energy into shifting into a better headspace.

When my children were younger and I was still getting the hang of this, I found that if I was feeling antsy because no one was really 'doing' anything, the best solution was for me to get out of everyone's space (where I was invariably making them feel antsy too). If I had some work to do, I might station myself at the kitchen table and let them know I was available if they needed me. Or I would get out some project of my own or tackle something in the garden. Invariably, things naturally shifted when I did this. Someone might wander into the kitchen to tell me something they'd just learned or to have a chat about some interesting thoughts they'd had. Or one would join me in whatever activity I was doing or feel inspired to dig out something interesting of their own. I clearly remember that sense of wonder at how easily things shift when you don't try to force them, and feeling slightly ridiculous that I had become so stressed in the first place.

Listen deeply

Perhaps you realize that you and your child need to talk something through or that you need to understand them better. Often, when we listen, our minds are on lots of other things – we're reactive to the words we hear or we're waiting to jump in with why we're right. When we practise mindful listening, we are listening from a place of presence, non-judgement and curiosity. It helps us to get below the surface and to communicate deeply. When we listen mindfully to our children, they are more likely to feel heard, understood and cared for.

There are many benefits to mindful listening:

- It enhances empathy and compassion, and the chance of us really understanding our child's perspective.
- It decreases tension in difficult conversations.
- It is nurturing for the relationship.
- It brings awareness to our own personal judgements, assumptions and biases.
- It serves as a model for your children for their future interactions.
- It helps us understand where our own boundaries are.

How to practise mindful listening

Mindful listening is about tuning in with the whole body, rather than only hearing what is said. Words are often just the surface and can easily be misinterpreted or have us jump to wrong or premature conclusions. When we listen and pay attention, we see many other cues, from our children and from ourselves:

1. *Find your ground and your 50/50.* Use the same process as for the 50/50 practice in Chapter 9 to find your ground, feeling into one of your anchors or your breath.
2. *Listen to the energy around your child's words.* Can you feel what emotions are present? Perhaps the words are angry or irritated, but what else is there? Sadness, frustration, worry, confusion?
3. *Be aware of what arises for you.* Pay attention to any impulses to interject with your own thoughts or experiences while your child is talking. Notice if your body responds to their words in some way, and what feelings are present for you: annoyance, stress, confusion, a desire to prove your point, or to present a solution?
4. *Let them know what you've understood.* When your child has finished speaking, let them know what you've understood. Be prepared for your child to be annoyed if you've got it wrong! In which case, and if it feels right to you, ask them for more information to deepen your understanding of their experience and point of view.

Even when things are really challenging, we can bring about big shifts by listening from this place of presence. In fact, these moments give us the opportunity to show our children that even the hardest emotions are okay to express. And that we can hold them in these emotions, even if we don't necessarily agree with them, or even if we also need to advocate for our own or someone else's needs.

Engaging with needs, not solutions

As you are listening mindfully, pay particular attention to any needs that your child may be expressing, directly or indirectly. A lot of conflicts tend to happen in families because we each present our solutions rather than our needs. For example, one person pushes for a family walk, another wants to spend the morning quietly playing with their LEGO® in their pyjamas, and another wants to go to the park and meet friends. If each person tries to convince the others that their solution is best, no one is likely to budge. It's a well-known fact about humans that when someone disagrees with us, we just dig our heels in deeper, or if we're a people-pleaser we might do it but won't feel satisfied and can burn out.

When we practise curiosity, on the other hand, we are more equipped to see the needs that drive those solutions, and when our language is needs-based rather than solutions-based, there is a far greater possibility that we reach a place of mutual understanding. The need to get out of the house and reconnect with nature to calm a busy mind, the need to feel safe and cosy after a difficult day, the need to connect with friends – these are universal needs that are likely to resonate and be understood by everyone. And if we all feel heard and respected, it is far easier to work together to find the path that honours all of us.

Responding to our children's needs helps them know they can express their needs

Parents often automatically assume that their solution is the best one, and that the plan they have created has to be the one that is followed. Consequently, children expressing their dissent is often interpreted as them being difficult or challenging. It may slow life down, but when our response is to take our children's needs seriously, we show them that their needs are important. And by encouraging them to express themselves in terms of needs and to hear others in the same way, we are helping them to take care of themselves while also being aware of the deeper needs of others.

> ❝ What she wants to do may be not the same as what I might have been thinking we could do. And in the past, I might have just thought no, that wasn't the plan. I've got much better at just pausing and thinking, could that be possible? And often it can be possible. It's recognizing

that ingrained hierarchy in the family where one person, because they're the parent, gets to decide what everyone's going to do. And realizing that children, if you allow them to have more autonomy, have often got really good ideas. That wouldn't have been something that I would have thought of, or that necessarily I would have put the same level of value on before." DONNA

Expressing our own needs

If you are used to putting everyone else's needs before your own, the last two chapters might well have revealed that it's time you started to speak up for yourself. This can be uncomfortable at first, but not only will it help you stay balanced, it's a fantastic way to model self-advocacy. When my children were small, I would find that when I was needed by more than one child at a time, my system went straight into overload and I would feel extremely irritable. Finally, I discovered that just letting everyone know that I was feeling a bit overwhelmed helped us all out. They understood and related to the concept of things just sometimes being a bit much, and they also understood that it wasn't anyone's fault. From there, it was often easy to find a solution, which might have been me just taking five minutes out, or us all figuring out what needed to be tended to first. It also meant that I gave my children the possibility of helping me, which they often did, by making a sweet suggestion or offering to come back later. Sometimes, of course, things didn't pan out quite so smoothly, but even then, just recognizing and expressing my needs was enough to stop any spiralling thoughts. My children also started to use the word 'overwhelmed' when their own nervous systems felt overloaded.

Some tips on communicating your needs

- *Avoid criticism and blame.* Focus on your own experience and needs rather than criticizing or blaming your child. Show your child that you take full responsibility for how you feel, and watch out in particular for them feeling guilty or hurt because they think they've done something wrong. Be aware that they may express this in a way that sounds defensive or angry.

- *Use neutral language.* Choose words that are neutral and non-judgemental to increase the likelihood that your child is receptive to you, and to reduce the possibility of them feeling criticized.

- *Use 'I' phrases.* Talk about you and how you feel, not what they or other people are doing.

- *Express your underlying needs.* If you desperately need some quiet space, don't focus on the solution (your child being quiet), but on why you need the quiet space, for example you have a lot on your plate, you didn't sleep well, you want to be well rested for some fun later on.

- *Check your non-language communication too.* My children are experts in spotting when my tone of voice doesn't match my words, and they can hear an edge no matter how emphatically I deny it. Facial expression, body language, tone and volume of voice – all these things will tell our children just as much as our words do. A mismatch can be extremely confusing to a child, so if they call you out on it, don't be afraid to admit that you are still feeling a little bit tense, or however you want to express it.

- *Stay present.* Focus on the current situation rather than bringing up past conflicts and grievances.

- *Be open to dialogue.* Be willing to engage in a dialogue with your child, and consider their needs and perspectives as well.

- *Be flexible.* Maybe your child has an idea of how your needs can be met that you hadn't thought of. Or maybe they have a solution that would work just as well as the solution you have in your mind. Be open to their suggestions.

- *Take a step back if you need to.* If, at any point, you notice that you are getting reactive, use one of the practices outlined earlier in this chapter to help you come back to your calm space again. It could be finding an anchor, a compassionate touch or simply taking a deep breath.

- *Be empathetic.* Show empathy for your child's feelings and needs, even if you don't understand them. Our aim is not to show how our need is more logical or must win the day, but to explore how we can work together to meet everyone's needs.

> " I am getting better at recognizing when I'm feeling that I need some time to myself, even if that means a solo trip to a coffee shop or taking myself off for a walk (usually while listening to an unschooling podcast!). This usually presents itself as feeling agitated or just plain old tired. I am also learning to 'cup fill' in the presence of my children. If they are happily busy at home, instead of hovering in case they need me, I will try and do something that I enjoy alongside them. I've found this so hard to do without feeling guilty, but I also recognize it does them both good to see me pursuing my own interests. I'm also finding that I am more honest with them now if I'm feeling overwhelmed or in need of a break. As we're with each other every day, looking after each other's emotional well-being is something that we talk about often." **ANNIE**

Fun and connection activities

I can't overstate the value of having things that you and your child love to do together. In moments when life feels a bit boring and no other idea quite hits the spot, or at times when, above all, you need to reconnect, these things that you both enjoy are fabulous for shifting everyone into a joyful frame of mind. They don't require you to plan anything or do something you don't really enjoy, and there is absolutely no higher purpose beyond feeling good.

Activities could be a dog walk with a flask of hot chocolate, a picnic in a nearby park, a stroll to a favourite shop, making cookies or having a disco in the kitchen. Our 'Fun and connection' activities list includes doing the rounds of the local charity shops in search of interesting things, walking one of the several dogs we borrow and ending with a milkshake at our favourite cafe, nipping to the beach for a quick swim, singing along to certain favourite tunes, and dancing in the kitchen to one of the songs from *Matilda*. The key to these activities is that they fill everyone's cups, they are financially accessible and they are easy to do spontaneously.

Journal prompts

- How does this new space feel for you? What differences do you notice from when you feel triggered?
- What new possibilities open up for you both in this space?
- What happens when you choose to do nothing?

Chapter summary

- Now that our old stories and fears are not running on autopilot, we are free to engage with the present moment in the way that is in the best interests of our child, ourselves and our relationship. This space feels radically different from the fight-or-flight space, both for us and for our children.

- Reconnecting with our child may sometimes be the best next step, and mindful listening allows us to deepen our understanding of their experience.

- Looking at the situation from the perspective of needs rather than solutions is extremely helpful for facilitating communication and understanding.

- If you realize that the fear is just something that you are imagining and ruminating on, think what you can do for yourself to shift your mood.

- There may be some action that needs to be taken to facilitate something new. And sometimes, a small shift in the environment can help to create a bigger shift in the mood.

Part 3

Nurturing yourself through change

The deep work required of us – and that we explored in Part 2 – has the potential to be profoundly transformative in your own life. By gently and consistently shifting your perspective and bringing compassion and curiosity to your self-inquiry, you are likely to observe changes across many areas of your life. Don't underestimate how challenging this might sometimes feel, or the importance of caring for yourself. In Part 3, we'll explore the ways these shifts may show up in your life, and look at all the ways you can make sure that you are supported along the way.

In the next three chapters we're going to look at how this process might unfold, daily practices to help you dig a little deeper, and the people and community that can support you as you steer your own life to a place that feels more coherent and authentic.

Chapter 12

Relearning to be yourself

Parents are frequently amazed by the depth of their own deschooling journey. As one father put it, 'I feel like it started out as a conversation about how to best learn maths, and it ended up as a reevaluation of my whole life.' We've seen throughout this book how our children reveal all the old stories that govern our lives and keep us trapped in patterns that no longer serve us. Our deschooling practice requires us to sit with all these patterns, and perhaps for the first time ever, to treat them kindly and to question them. This is a naturally healing process, and as we learn to respond in new ways, it is inevitable that our lives will shift and change far beyond the scope of our role as parents. As we work to get beyond our conditioning and accompany our children in their wholeness, we are naturally led towards our own wholeness.

Unravelling or peeling back the layers

I often think of the deschooling journey as a kind of unravelling. Everything seems so solid when we start out. There may be aspects of our lives that feel stuck and we may be wondering how we can make some changes. But generally, the concepts we've built our lives upon – the decades of conditioning, beliefs and patterns practised and repeated over and over – are bound up so tightly that we don't necessarily think to question them. Until, thanks to our children, we notice a stray end and tug at it gently. We realize that there are other ways of seeing and experiencing life, and we tug a little more. Slowly, those sturdy foundations start to unravel, like a ball of string. Other people describe this process as 'peeling back the layers', and I also love this image of a continual shedding of layer upon layer of 'shoulds' as we slowly return to our core.

Take your time

The other thing that parents discover is that this work never ends. In the beginning, it can be intense as your children present you with realization after realization. If you're anything like me, your first year will be spent furiously writing out the new waves of thoughts as they come crashing in, taking long, solitary walks every chance you can, and looking for like-minded people to talk to, all in the hope of finding some clarity. I also discovered in that first year that you can't force change. Sometimes, we have to unravel just a little more, or peel back a few more layers, before we can fully live into whatever new understanding we have come to. We may notice early on, for example, that we give little importance to our own needs, but it will probably take a while longer for us to understand what honouring our needs can look like and to give ourselves permission to do so.

Over time, the big 'aha' moments about yourself give way to gentler reflections. It becomes a way of life to notice what feels difficult, trust that you can work through it and come to the other side, a little bit wiser and a little bit more yourself. The tools become second nature, and turning to kindness and curiosity your new norm. The challenges and difficult moments still come, because life is never under our control, but you are far better equipped to surf the waves.

Why do our children lead us there?

There are several reasons that our children are such huge catalysts for our own change, and perhaps all are based on how they are unique in their ability to move us beyond conditioning and fear.

We're willing to be brave for them
Most of the parents I have spoken to will happily admit that if it wasn't for their child, they would never have found the courage to take a different path in life. While they may not have felt able to step up and advocate for themselves, they found that they were able to do that for their child. Following a deeper intuition, risking other people's disapproval or just entering unknown territory, things that felt too risky for themselves became possible when it was about their child's mental health and happiness, showing them they were capable of being far braver than they had ever dreamed.

Questioning the school system is a big deal
Reflecting on something that was almost certainly a formative part of our own lives, and which perhaps we had never questioned until now, is quite an undertaking, and will inevitably shake our foundations a little. Whether you enjoyed school or not, and whether you were quiet, compliant, chatty or rebellious, as you explore it in the context of your child, you will see your own experience through a more objective lens. This doesn't mean casting blame, or throwing negative light on things that were genuinely good. It simply means understanding how you interacted with school and learning, and what patterns you adopted to serve you best at the time. Having the ability to step back and look at such a key system through a new lens will give you the confidence to do the same with other systems in your life. Where do you feel more or less empowered? Where are you able to follow your internal navigation system, and where are you easily swayed by others? Where do you rebel, and where do you people-please?

> Throughout my life, I have always had a sense of what I should be doing or what I'm expected to do. And I think that takes you away from what you actually want to do. Whereas they know themselves really well, and they are just really clear about what they want to do and what they don't want to do." EVA

> I found myself questioning all the power and authorities I'd taken for

granted growing up. So I was like, hang on, how come you determine that we need to learn that tiny little slice? So it was about really learning to take responsibility for ourselves. They're following their natural paths and rhythms, and that's taught me that I can do the same. It has impacted every aspect of our lives. From recognizing our needs and wants at any given time to changing the way that we engage with the world. There has been a sense of immense freedom that has come from home education – a step towards what is really important, which is community, nature, joy and seeking what brings passion right now, rather than striving towards a future goal while suffering in the moment." NICOLA

They show us that we're wrong

As we watch our children learn and grow, we see that much of what we believe isn't the objective truth we once thought it was. Whether it's around how children learn, what they are capable of or what success looks like, our children will demonstrate over and over again that many of our beliefs are rooted in a place of fear. That when we let go of fear, all sorts of amazing things come into focus. And if that's true in one area of life, then perhaps, we think, it is also true in others.

We have to be coherent

I could always feel it in the pit of my stomach when I told my children it was okay to do something that actually I would have a hard time doing myself. Whether it was about following a passion, having a rest, setting boundaries or advocating for themselves, my conscientious, people-pleasing self – who struggled with all of those things – was painfully aware of her own hypocrisy. The thing is, though, that we have to try to live our lives in a way that is coherent with what we are saying to our children. And this is why our children are such a turbo-charged force for our own change. We are pushed out of our comfort zones far earlier and far more often than we would otherwise choose to be. So we really have no option but to fake it 'til we make it.

> You can say stuff to your kids until you're blue in the face, but if

you're not living that life, and they're not seeing you do that, then it's pointless. How can I be telling them to explore their passions and work through their frustrations if I'm not doing those things myself? I think it's so important to look at yourself as an adult and ask if you're living the life you really want to live. Firstly, do you know what you want? And secondly, are you actually taking action to live that life? Your kids need to see that. I've made more space for me and I've worked through a lot of the beliefs that were blocking me from pursuing my dreams, like feeling that I don't matter or that I can't ask for help." **CLAIRE**

They make us practise, day in, day out

The beauty and the challenge of deschooling is that multiple times a day our children require us to calm our nervous systems and lean in to what is happening. They show us that there is always something to learn, something to be grateful for, some little glimmer to see, something to get curious about. It's inevitable that as we hone our skills at continually grounding into the present moment and shifting our perspective, it becomes second nature to apply these skills to every corner of our lives.

Giving yourself permission

So in what ways might we give ourselves permission to be our whole selves? As we gently unravel, shedding the 'shoulds' as we go, and reconnecting with our own navigation system, we'll notice little shifts happening. We've spoken at length about how essential trust is to deschooling. As you learn to trust your children, you'll find that the doubtful voices in your head start to quieten, and that you are less easily thrown by outside opinions and expectations.

> It has affected every single area of my life. And every time I hit a part of my life that hasn't been touched by it yet, I know it's going to get there. It feels like you're just undoing a gazillion layers and unpicking a

hundred thorns. Every time you think you're done, it's like no, there's another one. It's affected how I live my day-to-day life, how I navigate through the world and all my relationships. That mindset that I don't have to follow rules that someone else made up. It's about thinking about what works for each person and in each moment. The gift of unschooling for me is that every time someone says 'should' or 'ought to' or 'must', there's a little question of 'Really? Is that true?' If you apply that to every part of your life, it's very freeing." HOLLY

" This whole process has made me realize how conditioned we are as a society. Families work so hard to put their kids through school, pay the mortgage and to ensure they have enough money to have family holidays every year. Unless you actively look for it, there's nothing to tell you that life doesn't have to be this way. Stepping out of the conventional way of doing things has meant that we are now a one-income family with less money but a whole new world has opened up to us. Not having the kids in school has meant we have so much more time together, and it really gets you thinking about living life in the moment as opposed to the end goal of getting your kids through school and then enjoying retirement." ANNIE

" I see it as a gift, even though I had feared it so much, because I see the world differently now. I hadn't realized how much I had been living in a kind of conditioned way of seeing the world. I had just aligned myself as somebody who follows the rules, doesn't break the law, doesn't do the wrong thing and just wants to please people. I've tried hard. I've studied hard. I've worked hard and I haven't always just really thought about what I want to do. What do I actually want to do? How would I actually like to spend my time if I wasn't thinking about the limitations. And that's what I love about what my daughter has shown me – that she just doesn't have the same limitations." DONNA

" We basically chucked our whole life up in the air. We had the four-bedroom house, the nice car and good jobs, but my husband and I were utterly miserable. We sold our house. We got off the housing ladder, which horrified my parents, and we went travelling for a little while. We have to keep flexing, and we have to keep moving, and it comes with its own challenges. But there's some freedom in that, and I don't think we'd have been able to do that if we hadn't gone through this process, because it seems like so much in life is binary. And actually, what we've realized with this is like, no, it's okay to question things. It's okay to say, this is what we want. To the outside, it might look like we're sacrificing everything for the children. But we're not. We're gaining such a lot by not being within that framework and that system." JAYNE

A few of the shifts you might spot taking place
Acknowledging that you are enough

We live in a society where the fear of not doing enough and not being enough is rampant. So much in our wider culture holds us in perfection-seeking patterns – how we do at school, how many friends we have, the job we do, the car we drive, how we look, how we dress etc. Some of these external indicators of success may be aligned with our own happiness and values, and some may not. By the time we are adults it can be hard to pick this apart because these success indicators are so deeply ingrained in our collective psyche. It becomes natural to project them onto our children and to push them to strive – partly to ensure that they are 'enough', and partly because we need to prove our 'enoughness' as parents. When you accept your child's enoughness just as they are and no longer project these fears onto them, you are likely to come to two conclusions. First, the times when you are feeling not enough will come into sharp focus. And second, you will realize that if your child is always enough, then surely you must be too.

> I had a chronic illness before this and judged myself harshly for not achieving more. Now I think more about who people are. I definitely question how we value people, and it's changed how I think about them. It's made me question why we measure people like we do and how I measure myself. I've never known my daughter as happy in these last two years, so none of it has to do with how much we do

but with who we are. I think more compassionately about myself now. I don't have an incredible career or go on lots of holidays, and I've made difficult choices, but they made me a better person." RHONDA

❝ It's definitely been healing. I'm so grateful that I was able to do this and that I was able to find the resources that I found at the time." HAYLEY

Understanding what makes you come alive

As you watch your child connect with their passions and joy, you'll see how certain things make them come alive. If, like many people, much of your life has been driven by what was expected of you and what made other people happy, then you may be struck by how essential these things are to your child. For many years, I didn't think much about my own joy, probably because I was far too busy doing and worrying about all the things I thought I was supposed to do and worry about. I was weighed down with so many responsibilities and obligations that I was hard-pressed to recognize what made me happy, never mind make it a priority.

The things we enjoy and feel passionate about are not just for fun, but are essential to our well-being and to our sense of self. Whether it's a sport, a creative endeavour, adventure, quiet time or meaningful work, activities that are fulfilling and joyful build our resilience and help us get through the more difficult moments. When you give your child permission to follow their heart, you may well start to see the things you do and the things you make time for in an entirely new light. You're likely to wonder if perhaps you have more choice and agency than you thought you did, and to realize that it is okay to give yourself permission to invest in the things you love.

❝ It feels exciting to explore what other changes we can make in our lives to get the most out of it. My husband, who has worked for the same company for over 20 years, said just yesterday that he's been thinking about how he could work to allow us to travel more as a family." ANNIE

> As they've grown older, what I need to respect is their space, so having my own work and passions really puts it all to the test. What do I love? How do I learn? What am I creating? If I believe that they can follow their passions, then I have to model that. When I'm busy and engaged in what I love, I think, well, this is all that we all want." **NICOLA**

Resting when you need to

I struggled for some years to model resting to my children. In my mind, being busy and active was good and healthy, whereas resting and 'not doing anything' was a bit of a waste of time. I also had some internalized mother guilt around allowing myself to rest. Watching my children figure out their rhythms and seeing how they often naturally resisted my attempts to cajole them into doing things forced me to take a long look at my own habits. Now if I'm tired I will have a guilt-free nap, and if I need an early night, I'll take it. Whereas, in my previous life, I would have run on empty for months, now I recognize when I am feeling depleted and need to slow life down a little. You'll know when you are truly valuing rest when you take a look at the week ahead, and instead of trying to fill it with things, you wonder if you planned enough downtime.

Setting boundaries and advocating for yourself

For parents who have been people-pleasers all their lives, understanding that they can set boundaries can be a real revelation. By encouraging our children to know their boundaries and advocate for themselves, we are likely to see places in our lives where we are not taking our own advice. Maybe we say yes to too many people, or we have a situation at work or in a relationship where our boundaries are frequently ignored, or where we feel incapable of advocating for ourselves. As we encourage our children to speak up, and choose not to value compliance over their autonomy, we will notice where in our own lives we tend to stay silent. And as we unpick the traditional power dynamics of parents and children, the relationships we have with people and systems that hold us in an imbalance of power will become painfully clear. Knowing what values we want to model to our children is likely to give us the motivation to take a stand, where in the past we may not have had the courage.

Valuing your own learning

It's a remarkable thing to watch a child delve freely into learning for the simple reason that they are interested in something. They don't worry about whether they are good or bad at that particular subject. They don't worry if they're learning enough. They don't worry about its perceived worthiness, or if it will get them somewhere. It doesn't occur to them that they won't be able to learn something. They just learn. You may well find yourself inspired by their confident, open-minded approach and open yourself to new learning opportunities.

> I'm as much a learner as she is. That's been a real gift from all of this, which I was not expecting. I've become a better learner. I've become much more open. In the pockets of time, where she's busy doing her thing, I've been able to go and pursue things that I'm more interested in. So I have this whole area of my life opening up that I just didn't have time for or didn't prioritize. Or somehow, maybe I just didn't think that was available to me. Or I didn't have the right teachers. I learned from her that I can just do it." DONNA

> The most unexpected learning was my own *un*-learning. Trusting my children meant observing how they thrived, and that made me question everything I believed about formal education. I had been a tryer at school, believing in rote learning and metered-out grade rewards. My children showed me how to really learn – through experience and joy. One of the greatest moments of understanding their learning was at their forest school one day when parents were invited to join a session. I watched a group of mixed-age children exploring ideas of community, gratitude and silence in nature and meditation, and I realized that it had taken me a cancer diagnosis and 40 years of age to feel that I had the space to explore these concepts." NICOLA

Seeing the world differently

As we let go of our social conditioning, accepting our children for who they are, and not trying to make them anything that anyone else says they should be, we are likely to see the world through a different lens. We realize that it is not true that children, unless cajoled, praised or punished, would never do anything and never get anywhere. Instead, we observe that when people's needs are met, they are far more likely to be deeply motivated, compassionate and cooperative. We're not meant to be the same, but we are meant to work together with the gifts we each have.

> I think it makes you a much more generous person to other people in terms of understanding that there's no one right way to live a life. It feels like a gift of seeing everyone through the most positive lens that you can. Everyone is just doing their best all the time with what they have." HOLLY

> Doing this has helped me to see when I don't live according to my own values. She'll pull me up when I'm not being coherent, so I have to think about that and recognize it. I think a lot about our own individual human natures and what we're all asking and looking for. What this has really given me is the realization that people are made to be cooperative, kind and compassionate. It isn't just an ideal. When we're given autonomy and left to do things in our own time, we naturally choose to be happy, to be helpful and to cooperate." LIANNE

Working with our practical limitations

As our children keep pushing us up against new learning edges, and we understand more about ourselves and how we want to live, we may also bump up against the practical limitations of our lives right now. It's an odd contradiction that while we are so involved with our children we are also learning more about who we are and how we want to move in the world. And understanding how we can be our whole selves within this framework may feel like a bit of a puzzle to solve. Although not always the case, it is often the mother who does the lion's share of accompanying the children, understanding their needs and working out how to meet them. This in itself is a challenge in many families, and casting a compassionate and curious, unschooling eye over expectations and roles can be a constructive approach to working out if the setup feels healthy and coherent for everyone. Whichever parent or caregiver you are, it's important to recognize what your evolving needs are beyond your children, and as best as possible within the limitations that exist, find ways to meet and honour them.

> ❝ I feel like it's almost a contradiction sometimes. We want to model to our children the best way to live, but then the fact that you're with your children all day may be also making that harder. I'm a complex human and I have other things that are interesting in my life and things that I want to think about. Just because motherhood and home education are where I am right now doesn't mean that there isn't any more to me, or that I don't need things for myself." JAYNE

Applying Self-Determination Theory to ourselves

In Chapter 2 we looked at Self-Determination Theory as a framework within which to consider our children's needs. It's also a helpful framework for looking at our own lives and understanding where we may need to pay some more attention. Think about the three main needs that we all need to meet to thrive in life: autonomy, competence and connection. How well are you meeting yours?

Autonomy: Do you feel like you're in control of your own life? Or does it feel like other people are calling all the shots?

Competence: Do you feel like you're using your gifts, and engaging and learning about things that make you feel alive? Are you managing to balance parenting with what it means for you to feel purposeful in the world?

Connection: Do you have enough meaningful connections available to you? Do you feel seen and appreciated by those around you?

Taking the journey together

Like most parents, Claire had never intended to unschool, but realized it was the only way forward for her sons after a stressful and challenging time at school. She didn't expect it to have the profound effect that it did on her own life. Claire describes how choosing to trust her children and to journey alongside them led her to question many aspects of how she had been living. She learned to be more gentle with herself, and to question the things that no longer felt coherent. This process of trusting her children alongside her own self-enquiry led to many shifts, from relearning to trust in her own intuition, and delving deeper into her own passions, to challenging her own people-pleasing tendencies.

> My intuition has come back through this whole process and I feel like I'm a completely different person. I have so much trust and belief now in myself and my children. I had a situation recently in my wider family that I had to deal with and, after a difficult meeting with a solicitor, my brother said how grateful he was that I could cut through all the noise and just move things forward. It's like I'm finally going, 'This is me, world' and everyone else is saying, 'Okay, she's got this', whereas the old me would have said, 'Don't take up the space.' I think it's really important that you show up fully as yourself and allow other people to give you your space.
>
> I get sad sometimes because I feel like I made so many mistakes

and I wish I could take me now and plonk me back at the beginning of parenting. But that's life – we can only do our best. It blew my mind when I took them out of school because I'd been the eternal good girl, and this felt really naughty. But once I did it I thought, well, the world hasn't blown up. We're told that they have to go to school, but in fact the world was still turning and everything was fine. I began to wonder what else wasn't true, and I was quite thrown for a while at how there are so many things in our lives that we're told should be a certain way. Now instead, as a family we are looking beyond what society deems you are supposed to do in order to be successful, and instead choosing a life that works for us.

I think I was quite lost and I didn't really know what brought me joy. I was stuck in that place of earning the gold star. I had to figure out what intrinsically brings me joy rather than seeking external validation where someone else tells me I've done well. I was asking my children to tell me what their passions were, but I didn't know my own, so I was really going on that journey alongside them, finding out together and having fun doing that. Slowly, over time, I found that I love physical labour. At school I was seen as quite academic, so I probably got pushed down that route. But actually I get joy from digging in the garden, and doing DIY. I think we often just get to surface level and we think we just need a bath or a massage. We've got to really go deep to find what fires us up." CLAIRE

Journal prompts

- As you deschool, what shifts are you noticing in the way you see your life?
- What old beliefs and stories are you starting to question?
- What new ways of being are starting to feel possible?

Chapter summary

- Parents often find their deschooling journey profoundly transformative, reaching far beyond parenting and education and influencing many facets of their lives.

- Deschooling involves a gradual unravelling of old habits and beliefs. Initially intense, it eventually becomes a lifelong practice of noticing our learning edges and working through them.

- Our children are instrumental in giving us the courage and context to confront our old conditioning and fears, and to prompt deep reflections on the way we are conditioned and on the systems and relationships that we are part of.

- Through deschooling, many ways we live are likely to shift, from valuing rest and setting boundaries to advocating for ourselves and making our happiness a priority.

- We may need to figure out how we can live fully into our own lives while also holding our children in theirs.

Chapter 13

Practices to support you in your deschooling journey

Throughout this book, we've explored how we can bring about change by intentionally addressing our old stories and fears as they arise. This will sometimes feel exhilarating, sometimes insurmountable, and sometimes just plain exhausting. My own deschooling journey began after several years of mindfulness practice, and I was still amazed by how often and how powerfully I was triggered, and how much energy it took to keep just working through it all. And, as we saw in the last chapter, your work will naturally spill into other areas of your life, creating endless new opportunities and challenges.

The more familiar we become with our nervous systems, and the more adept at identifying and navigating old patterns, the easier our deschooling becomes. Incorporating additional practices into your daily life to support you in building these capacities is incredibly helpful. You'll probably find that you are naturally drawn towards what you need, whether that is quiet space to ponder and chew over your thoughts, more intentional mindfulness practices that help you stay calm in difficult moments, or cultivating your ability to find joy in your days. In this chapter, you'll find different practices you can easily bring to your daily life and which will help to smooth the rough edges of your deschooling journey.

Why do we need specific practices?

While we're still grappling daily with doubts and fears, and perhaps with those of people around us, we'll find that our levels of confidence fluctuate wildly. This is particularly relevant in the leap-of-faith period, when old paradigms are beginning to fall but we haven't yet replaced them with something new. Practices that are designed to help us stay calm and present can help us build a more solid foundation. This doesn't mean that the ups and downs of life won't happen, but as we feel more grounded and trusting, we will be less at the mercy of our volatile thoughts and more able to reconnect with our own navigation system.

Capacities to cultivate
Here are some capacities we can cultivate through daily practice:

- identifying our fears and their origins
- increasing our ability to recognize old patterns in the body
- staying regulated and calm
- allowing ourselves to feel more joy in the present moment.

Making time for yourself
You don't need to find an extra hour every day for these practices, and nor should you add them to your to-do list and then feel guilty for not doing them. However, making time for things that benefit you is an important part of deschooling. First, because these practices will create more space in your life and make the whole process much easier. Second, because showing our children how we support ourselves is important because it tells them that they too can invest time in doing the things that support them. And last, because despite whatever we have subconsciously learned about being a parent, there is no reason to feel guilty about giving ourselves time for the things we need.

Some of the practices can be built easily into the day, some you can do with your child if they're on board with it, and others may require you to find some quiet time. So play around and find which ones feel the most helpful to you, and then see how you can incorporate them into your life. You may have other practices of your own that you find useful too.

> ❝ Yoga, going to the woods by myself. Sometimes you think you need a month in Barbados, but in fact just 10 minutes in the woods is enough to reset. You can't not afford to take your time out and do your practices. Even just asking for 10 minutes for yourself and showing them how you do that. If we want them to care for themselves, then we need to show them how to do it." LIANNE

Plan your week

It can be helpful to look at your week ahead and consider where there might be pockets of time for some of the deeper practices or for calm reflection. Can you get up a little earlier than your child? Are there activities they do when you could carve out time for yourself? Are there quiet times of the day that you could make the most of? Be aware of anything that comes up for you as you look at the week ahead – guilt, a sense of not deserving, resentment at lack of time or a feeling that you should be doing something else instead, for example. Try bringing kindness and curiosity to these feelings, and see if you can unpick them a little more.

Contemplative activities

What activities naturally quieten your mind? It can feel radical to stop and make time for these things, but they are key to creating that solid foundation.

Time in nature

There is now a wealth of research that shows how spending time in nature brings numerous benefits to our physical and mental well-being. It reduces stress levels by lowering cortisol, enhances our mood through increasing serotonin, and boosts our focus and concentration. Even a brief nature break of just 15 minutes can improve our overall well-being, acting as a quick recharge for body and mind. Some children may love heading out for adventure, whereas others may be less keen, so get creative if you need to. Do you have a short walk near your home that you could do by yourself? Could you find alternative ways to go to and from activities to incorporate a stroll through a park? Could you make this a win-win by finding nature-based activities that might also appeal to your child or that involve friends?

50/50 nature practice

Alone or with your child, you can enhance the benefits of your time in nature by making it a practice in mindful awareness.

1. Take a couple of deep breaths and connect with your body through the anchor practice, and let your senses come alive.
2. Close your eyes if it's safe to do so, and notice the sounds around you – bird song, leaves crunching underfoot, rustling of the trees. Feel the air on your skin, noticing if it's chilly and damp, or if you feel a breeze or the warmth of the sun.
3. Take another deep breath in and smell the fresh air and scents.
4. Then, keeping your awareness in your body, open your eyes and look around as if you can were seeing it all for the first time. Notice the colours, the patterns, what moves and what stays still, any flowers or plants you may have never seen before. Reach out to touch what's near you and notice how it feels– the bark of a tree, a smooth rock, a flower. If you're on grass, you might like to walk barefoot or even just lie on the grass, paying attention to how it feels. Notice how your body responds to this practice and how your mood shifts.

Journalling

Journalling can be an excellent companion to your deschooling and a valuable tool for self-discovery. Through the process of putting our thoughts on to paper, we can gain new insights into our patterns and triggers. And journalling gives us a little distance from our difficult experiences and emotions, helping us work through them in a safe and structured way. It also allows us to look at an event or thoughts from multiple perspectives and add in some hindsight, helping us see it in a far more nuanced way. Reading back over entries from six months or a year ago can also be immensely reassuring as it shows you how far you've come. And if you don't have anyone to share in-depth with, journalling can also be a welcome and necessary emotional release.

> In the early days, I journalled a lot. It felt like my head was very full, so just getting everything down onto the page was really good for me. I would do it when I could feel in my body that I wasn't really okay, and then I would write everything down. Then I could start to see more of what was going on. When I write, things will jump out of the page at me, or I can ask 'Is that really true?' I still get stuck in my head sometimes." CLAIRE

Morning Pages

For the first two years after our sons left school, my first stop in the morning was my notepad and pen. I found the practice of Morning Pages (popularized by Julia Cameron in her book *The Artist's Way* (1995)[1]) extremely helpful. Rather than the more considered process of journalling, Morning Pages involves writing three pages of stream-of-consciousness first thing in the morning, and before the prefrontal cortex has come online to start filtering things out. It's a wonderful way to access thoughts and fears that might be hidden under other layers. The unfiltered nature of this kind of writing allows for free expression and a more organic exploration of ideas. Pay attention to the energy around what you're writing. I would invariably find that I might start with something trivial or banal, but my writing would always head in a direction that was helpful to me. You may want to hold on to your writing for a while, but since the true value of this work is in the process itself, you may equally prefer to throw the pages away, or even ceremoniously burn them.

---

1   See https://juliacameronlive.com/basic-tools/morning-pages

Mindful meditation

As you deschool, you'll be intentionally bringing mindfulness to many moments in your days and, over time, this approach will become second nature. It will become normal for you to look for calm in your body, to figure out what's going on for you, to listen deeply to your child and to find a way to meet their needs while also meeting your own. These simple mindful steps repeated multiple times a day will, over time, create deep shifts in your life.

You can strengthen your mindfulness muscle by incorporating some simple meditation practice into your life. Just 10 to 15 minutes a day will help you learn how to more easily quieten your thoughts and reach for that place of connection and trust. You'll become more able to discern when you are triggered and what you need, and the practice of continually reaching for the present moment will help you find the present moment during your days with your child.

The key to mindful meditation is to approach it with an open and curious mind, allowing yourself to be present with whatever arises, without judgement. Lots of people say they can't meditate because they can't stop the stream of thoughts. In fact, the practice is to keep noticing when your mind has drifted and to come gently back to the breath. So if your mind keeps wandering, be gentle with yourself and remind yourself that not only is this normal, but that this is exactly the practice.

How to meditate, in five steps

1. *Find a quiet and comfortable space.* Choose somewhere where you won't be disturbed, and sit or lie down in a comfortable position. This could be cross-legged on a cushion, in a chair with your feet flat on the ground, or lying down on a yoga mat.
2. *Set a time limit.* It can be easier in the beginning to set a timer. Try starting with 10 minutes.
3. *Focus on your breath.** Soften your gaze or close your eyes, and then take a moment to check in with how you are. Do you feel calm and present, or is your mind preoccupied with something

in the day ahead or something that happened yesterday? What's the feeling tone of this moment? Bring your attention to your breath, noticing its rhythm and sensations as you inhale and exhale – the air in your nostrils, the rise and fall of your chest and belly.

4. *Be present.* Your mind will almost certainly wander. Instead of wrestling with your thoughts, or trying to stop them, just practise coming gently back to your breath whenever you become aware of the wandering. As hard as it may seem, that's all there is to this. You don't need to try to eliminate or block your thoughts. Simply observe them without judgement and keep coming back to your breath over and over again. Labelling thoughts as 'thinking' can help you recognize them as passing events in the mind rather than getting caught up in them. Or try imagining them as clouds passing by in the sky.

5. *End with gratitude.* Gently bring your awareness back to your surroundings, wiggle your fingers and toes, and slowly open your eyes. Take a few deep breaths and carry the sense of calm and presence you've cultivated into the rest of your day. Take a moment to express gratitude for this time you've set aside for yourself. Even if you feel like you spent 10 minutes just bringing your wandering mind back!

* If you prefer, you can use one of the anchors we explored in Chapter 8. So, rather than coming back to the breath, come back to the feet or the hands.

Walking meditation

The name may conjure up images of Zen monks gliding through a peaceful garden, but in fact you can do this anywhere that you can walk fairly slowly, and no one will take a second glance. Something valuable that walking meditation brings is the ability to be connected with ourselves while also fully immersed in the world around us. Remember the 50/50 practice from Chapter 10? Walking meditation will improve your capacity to be with yourself and your child at the same time. You can do the practice for any length of time that feels comfortable for you.

1. *Bring your awareness to your body and breath.* Start by standing still for a moment and bringing your awareness to your body. Notice your posture and feel the weight of your feet on the ground. Bring your attention to your breath.
2. *Begin to walk slowly.* Pay attention to each step you take. Feel the sensation of your feet lifting off the ground, moving forward, and making contact with the ground again. You can synchronize your breath with your steps if that helps you stay focused.
3. *Bring your awareness to your walking.* Bring your attention to the physical sensations of walking. Notice the movement of your muscles, the shifting of your weight from one foot to the other, and the feeling of the ground beneath your feet. Stay present with each moment of the walking process.
4. *Notice your surroundings.* While walking, remain aware of your surroundings without getting caught up in them. Notice the sights, sounds and smells around you, but gently guide your focus back to the sensations of walking whenever your mind starts to wander.
5. *Notice your thoughts and emotions.* Acknowledge any thoughts or emotions that arise, but don't dwell on them. Simply let them pass and return your focus to the present moment and the sensations of walking.
6. *End your walking meditation.* When you're ready to end your walking meditation, gradually slow down your pace. Come to a stop and take a moment to stand still, just as you did at the beginning. Reflect on your experience and how you feel after the practice.

Mindful movement

Mindful movement practices, such as yoga, tai chi or qi gong, bring us the same benefits as mindful meditation, with the added bonus that we get some exercise at the same time. If you find it hard to sit still, mindful movement may feel easier to access than meditation. And if you are with a young child, they may find it entertaining enough to join in. If you aren't able to attend classes, you could find online videos to follow in your sitting room. Alternatively, simply roll out a mat and dedicate a few minutes to some mindful stretching, incorporating whatever stretches feel comfortable and right for you.

> ### Some tips for mindful stretching
>
> - *Stay present.* Focus on the sensations in your body and your breath.
>
> - *Move slowly.* Avoid rushing through the stretches. Move slowly and mindfully, listening to your body.
>
> - *Breathe deeply.* Use your breath to deepen the stretches and release tension.
>
> - *Respect your limits.* Never push your body into pain. Remember that the emphasis is on staying present, not pushing your physical limits.

If you do any other exercise during the week, such as running, swimming or cycling, you can also bring this same quality of mindfulness to it by using your breath as an anchor and focusing your awareness on the sensations in the body as they shift and change.

Finding flow

The concept of 'flow' was introduced by psychologist Mihaly Csikszentmihalyi in the 1970s, and has since been influential in many fields, including psychology, education and sports (Csikszentmihalyi 1975). Flow happens when we are fully absorbed in an activity we enjoy, and it's characterized by intense focus, loss of self-awareness and a sense of time distortion. With its focus on the present moment, research shows that flow brings similar health benefits to those of mindfulness.

The key to entering flow state is to find an activity you love, and then pitch it at the right skill level. If it's too easy, you're likely to get bored, and if it's too difficult, you'll probably feel some tension. The activity that works for you could be anything from gardening to swimming, playing the guitar or writing. I've always found that certain crafts are my go-to for entering flow state. When I'm engaged in making something with my hands, any noise in my brain immediately quietens.

You may have noticed how and when your child accesses flow state, and how deeply they can be involved in an activity they're doing. Interestingly, there is burgeoning research that shows how some video games also encourage a flow state of mind, and are helpful in alleviating anxiety and depression (Khoshnoud, Alvarez Igarzábal and Wittmann 2020).

Incorporating flow into your life

You may need to get creative about incorporating more flow into your life. If you are fortunate enough to share a love for something with your child, then doing that together is clearly a win-win. Bear in mind that if they don't find the activity quite as engaging as you do, or if the skill level isn't pitched just right for them, they're unlikely to get into any kind of flow. In which case, your experience is unlikely to be quite so mindful! It may be more realistic to have something that you can go to when your child is engaged in something else. If they're playing with LEGO® or immersed in Minecraft, that could be a perfect moment to pick up whatever project you have at hand.

Finding a flow activity to turn your attention to when you are triggered or anxious is also a great way to soothe your nervous system. Activities that have a repetitive motion, such as knitting, are particularly effective for reducing anxiety.

Mindful moments

Introducing regular mindful moments into your life will help you hone the ability to move out of your busy mind and reconnect with your body. This practice also reminds us how rich the present moment always is if we can just sink into it and get curious. You could use any daily activity for this, but brushing your teeth is a particularly good one, for its regularity and repetitive nature.

1. Start by bringing your attention to the present moment. Feel the texture of the toothbrush in your hand, and the colour and smell of the toothpaste. Tune in to how the toothpaste tastes as you put the toothbrush in your mouth and you start to brush. You don't need to overthink any of these things – just register how they feel.
2. As you begin brushing, focus on the sensations: the movement of your arm, the feeling of the toothbrush against your teeth, and the touch of the bristles on your gums.
3. Every time your mind wanders, gently bring it back to these sensations. Avoid rushing, and instead be present with each stroke.
4. When you finish the practice, take a moment to notice how you feel.

Mindful self-care

Approaching self-care from a perspective of mindfulness ensures we're doing things for the right reasons. Exercise and eating are good examples of this, where there are just so many places where we can easily get rigid and self-critical. We can strive, punish ourselves if we get it wrong, feel shame, compare ourselves to others or criticize ourselves for being lazy.

If, on the other hand, we come to self-care from a place of Being rather than Doing, we'll be more able to gently tune in to see what our bodies need, whether that is rest, food or exercise. By becoming more mindful, we're likely to find that our body naturally starts to guide us towards what it needs, rather than having to make a forced effort with our minds. Sometimes, we might find that we are resistant to giving ourselves what we need, in which case we can bring that lens of self-compassion and curiosity to whatever reason we have that makes us feel unable to take good care of ourselves. Perhaps our week is not nourishing enough, and we are feeling a little depleted. Perhaps we can engage in a short mood-shifting activity instead of coming down hard on ourselves. Perhaps it's a sign that we need to make some kind of change in our lives.

Other practices we can bring to our lives

Celebrate completion

Life and parenting are never done. No matter how hard we work, there is always the next thing to do or achieve, so we rarely sit back and celebrate the milestones. Not only that, but we tend to overestimate what is still to be done while underestimating our achievements. Have you ever had a week ahead with so many monumental things to sort and do that you didn't think you'd make it through 'til Sunday? Then you did make it through, but after a quick sigh of relief, you probably found yourself already immersed in worrying about the next set of challenges looming. Living like this can feel relentless and as though we're just treading water. Acknowledging when we've achieved things, risen to difficult challenges, or just managed to claw our way through helps to combat negativity bias, increase our self-confidence and keep self-sabotaging thoughts at bay.

So take a moment to celebrate your achievements and your breakthroughs, however small they would seem to the outside world. Marking the moment may just mean going for a walk or a coffee, taking a few minutes to journal about it or announcing it to a supportive friend. Whatever you choose to do, allow yourself a pat on the back and bask a little in your own glory.

Start the day well

First thing in the morning, we have the opportunity to set the tone for the day. That's not to say that the tone will necessarily last us all day, but bringing intention to these first moments is still extremely helpful. When we wake up, our minds have a tendency to go straight back to the things we were worrying about yesterday, but there's a little window of time we can catch before this happens. A simple practice is to take three deep breaths as soon as you wake up, and then set an intention for the day. Allow your intention to tap into your wider deschooling aims. For example, 'Today, I will prioritize my relationship with my children above everything else', 'Today I will tend to myself first if I feel anxious', or 'Today, I will look for all the joyful moments.'

Gratitude practice

Research shows that people who regularly practise gratitude are far more likely to be able to hold their ground in a stressed moment. Just like meditation, the practice of gratitude affects our body's chemistry, decreasing stress hormones and activating the brain stem to produce dopamine. The short-term result is a reduction in anxiety and an improvement in mood. In the long term, regularly practising gratitude improves our immune systems and makes us more resilient to the ups and downs of life.

Ten mindful fingers gratitude practice

The best time to practice this is at the end of each day.

1. *Bring awareness to your body.* Take a moment to ground into your body, using the anchors or your breath.
2. *Check in with yourself.* Practising gratitude is not the same as forced positive thinking. There's nothing wrong with a positive attitude, but we have to be careful not to push difficult feelings away by coating them in a layer of positivity. So always check in first with how you are. Notice the feeling tone of this moment – the thoughts, feelings and sensations that are present. If you are feeling challenged in any way, use a self-compassion practice to touch in gently with those feelings and with your needs.
3. *Count things you're grateful for.* Bring your attention to 10 things in your day that you're grateful for, using each finger to say to yourself or out loud, 'I am grateful for...'. These may be big, important things, or they may just be small moments in the day

that you might ordinarily not even notice – the sun shining, the comfortable chair you're sitting in or a text from a good friend.

Keep your cup filled!

It's a common irony that when life feels challenging, we give up the very things that nourish us. These are often the first to go, because we feel like we don't have time for them, or we feel guilty about doing things just for us. The problem is that when we stop doing the little things that make life feel rich and meaningful, we feel less joy in our daily lives, increasing the stress and feeding into the narrative that now we really don't have time for such luxuries. Not only do the fun, joyful things help us stay fulfilled and happy, but what better way to encourage your child to do new and interesting things than to model that yourself?

What do you love to do? And are you giving yourself permission to do it? Whether it's coffee with friends, cold water swimming, a craft, dancing or amateur dramatics, show your child that happiness matters. How would we like them to live? Too busy or guilty to invest time in the things they love? Or making sure that their lives are balanced and taking care to keep their cup filled?

> " Hanging out with friends with children fills my cup. Having the kids play and to be able to talk with other mothers and adults. Dancing in my kitchen fills my cup. If I can't do anything, or it's raining and no one is coming over, I'll dance every day as it gives me a big boost." HOLLY

> " I paint and do various crafts. I'm also starting to write more because it helps me organize my thoughts and explore my own experiences. And I'm taking more time out for myself. I think that, within our couple, I took on too much of the responsibility at home, so I'm in the process of taking some of that back. So I'm going away for the weekend to stay with a friend. Last weekend I took myself to the cinema. It's very easy to not find that time. That's something I'm working on at the moment." JAYNE

Creating new habits

We've discussed at length how our brains are naturally wired to keep returning to what's familiar. This is why it often takes time for new practices to become established as daily habits. In the beginning, you may struggle to stick with these practices consistently, or find that, amid the busyness of daily life, you sometimes just forget about them altogether. With time and consistency, however, you'll start to look forward to the things that keep you feeling nourished and balanced, and to notice when you've gone a day or two without filling your own cup. Be patient with yourself, and remember that it takes a while to discover which practices work best for you and for them to become a natural, enjoyable part of your daily life.

Here are a few practical tips to make things easier:

1. *Start small and realistic.* Avoid being over-ambitious. Start instead by choosing something you can integrate fairly easily into daily life without needing to shift lots of things around. The more complicated it is, the less appealing it is likely to feel. Ten minutes of meditation on the sofa may well be far more achievable than an hour-long yoga class, for example.

2. *Use habit stacking.* Make new habits easier to remember by linking them to an existing routine. This is often called 'habit stacking' – one habit triggers the next. For example, you could journal while drinking your morning coffee, or practise a brief meditation after putting your child to bed. Attaching new habits to familiar activities helps create consistency.

3. *Practice self-compassion.* Building habits takes time, and research suggests it can take at least two months for new routines to become automatic. If you miss a day or two, don't feel discouraged. Instead, simply pick up where you left off, focusing on progress over perfection.

4. *Create accountability.* Having support from a friend, family member or partner can be extremely motivating. If possible, find someone with similar goals to practise alongside or encourage you. Accountability partners can provide gentle reminders, and make the journey of building new habits feel less isolating.

Journal prompts

- Which practices do you feel would benefit you most?

- How can you incorporate these into your days? Can someone help you? Is there something you could reorganize?

- Do you feel any resistance to giving yourself this time? If so, what might you need to hear in order to give yourself permission?

Chapter summary

- There are many daily practices that can support our deschooling, by deepening our ability to regulate our nervous system and increasing the joy in our daily lives.

- Mindful practices can include meditation, journalling, yoga and engaging in 'flow' activities.

- Planning and integrating these practices into daily routines without guilt is essential, and sets an example for our children.

- Celebrating completion, starting the day well and gratitude practice all help us maintain a healthy and balanced mindset.

- When we are busy or tired, it's easy to forget the very things that make our lives fun and fulfilling or to feel like we don't have time for them. This can create a vicious circle, leading to further depletion.

Chapter 14

Creating your community

For many families, the shift to living without school involves significant upheaval. For some, it may mean one partner giving up work, with all the financial implications that brings. Others might change their working hours to allow for tag-teaming or find work that enables one parent to work from home. Some families downsize their home or move to be nearer relatives who can lend a hand. For single parents, the logistics can be particularly challenging and are likely to require a lot of juggling. Leaving a community, changing jobs, putting some plans on hold for a while – whatever adjustments you have to make to your family life, it can take time for things to fall into place. Even after the dust has settled, there will be days when everything flows beautifully and days where things feel quite difficult. Although there is plenty of work we can do with our own thoughts and feelings, it's also essential that we take a look at our lives and make sure we have the outer scaffolding in place too. While we hold space for our children, we might ask ourselves 'What holds us?'

Whenever I chat with other parents whose children aren't at school, we almost always end up talking about community. At the heart of self-directed learning is really the idea of a healthy community – different people living together as their full selves while respecting and honouring each other's differences and boundaries. And yet, choosing not to go to school sometimes means leaving or not entering the only community a family has easy access to. It's a paradox that one of the values many parents often hold most dear can also be the most elusive and frustrating.

> "Community is the biggest thing for unschooling, preferably in person, but even online. Just some people who you can share your biggest fears with, your worst days with, your celebrations and your triumphs. Just having a companion on the path with you. It's not always perfect, so sometimes someone to stop and look at the beautiful view with you and say 'Look, look what we've done.' Or someone to pick you up when you fall over and you're wondering how you're ever going to make it. You need those people." HOLLY

We're hard-wired for community

Feeling like we're part of a community is good for us. Social connection makes us feel safer and more fulfilled, helps us regulate our emotions, and even improves our immune systems. When we feel isolated and disconnected from others, we are more prone to anxiety and depression, and even our physical health can take a hit. It's also obvious to most parents that this was never meant to be done in isolation. Even though it is very much the norm now, any person who has ever had to spend a day juggling the multiple commitments of children, work and home knows that it makes no sense at all, and that the village we all dream of is mostly absent from modern life.

In the context of a society in which community has generally been devalued, school offers a ready-made community. Even when things aren't going well, it's natural for there to be some sense of belonging and of a common, shared experience. Many parents are not prepared for the sense of loss that can hit them when they leave that community. What felt like a great decision at the start of summer can often feel quite different in September as the days get shorter and the parks empty of children. Alongside the relief of leaving whatever the struggles were, there can be a sense of real overwhelm as they face the formidable responsibility of creating something new. I vividly remember our first September day at home, many years ago. Our house was just a block from the school that my sons had been attending. Despite it being a conscious choice to leave, I felt my heart lurch at the sound of parents and children passing by on their first day back to school. It didn't make me feel excited by our newfound freedom; it just made me feel alone and a little fearful of the path ahead.

Stepping away to become the odd one out can feel extremely vulnerable. And there is likely to be an awkward transition period as you figure out who and where your new community is.

> We felt like part of something quite nurturing at primary school, and I felt a sense of loss of community as soon as my daughter stopped being able to attend. There was always something going on that you could be involved in. The moment she stopped attending it was a massive shock to the system. The school didn't seem to care, which was really harsh, and I started to wonder if it really was a nurturing community, as it had only worked when my child was able to be on their terms and not when she was struggling. I remember crying about this." RHONDA

> Coming out of school, I probably did lose contact with a lot of people, and that was hard. Some people weren't okay with our choice and I had to learn to let that go." CLAIRE

It can feel lonely in the beginning, but avoid daydreaming

If you've had to make changes in your work, you might also be mourning the loss of more time with other adults during the day and finding that your own social needs are no longer being met. To work your way through the challenges of deschooling in the beginning while feeling isolated is difficult. With no one to share stories with or to reassure you, you may be prone to seeing your days through a more negative lens, and you might even give yourself a hard time for not feeling delighted at being with your children all day. Don't beat yourself up or feel like you've made a mistake. Just see if you can sit with the discomfort and use it as valuable information to figure out what you and your children do need. Remember that it can take a little while to build something new.

In the early days, I often daydreamed about living in some Utopian community where children and adults spend their days happily getting on with life, helping each other out and learning together. Dreams are great if they're moving us towards what we want, but if they just set the bar impossibly high, they can also lead us to feeling dissatisfied with what we have. So if you find yourself wishing things looked different, it's fine to acknowledge that this isn't easy, and to feel annoyed that modern life is just not well set up for this. But then see what's around you and if there is something you can do right now to inch your way towards the community you need. What connections do you already have that you can nurture? What other connections could you put some energy into?

> "I had hoped that we would join home education groups, and I did think that that would be brilliant and wonderful, and it didn't happen. That was another thing I had to let go of. So because we live rurally, and I haven't been able to leave the children, I've brought community to me. In September, I started a mother's circle, which has been brilliant. I brought other women who are doing something similar, and we come and sit together and talk and share what's going on, how we are, and celebrate what's going well, and that feels really positive. It tops me up. We all get it, and other people bring something totally spontaneous and joyful that happened, and we can all really feel inspired and infused, going back and looking for these small moments. Often it's just finding ways of looking at the small everyday moments and realizing that's where life is happening." DONNA

Building a community for you and your children

Be intentional about your community

The beautiful thing is that from this unsettling space, you have the chance to build something intentional for you and your children. Rather than feel down about what you feel you might be missing, talk with your children and see what matters to you all, and then look at ways to bring that into your lives. You may be fortunate and find that there is a local home ed community that you can slot right into, but this may well not be the case. Far more likely is that the community you build will be a hodgepodge network of connections and friendships forged through shared activities, special interests, local events and friends of friends. Your community may well be made up of people of all ages and from all walks of life. And it will look nothing like school.

> And actually, lots of our people are also at school. I think you need some unschooling friends because otherwise you're on your own, but not all of them have to be. You just need people who support you and understand that what you're doing is right for your family, and who you can talk to without judgement." **HOLLY**

It's a slow and organic process that's always changing and evolving

Accept that building your community is likely to be a slow and organic process. It will probably take a lot of effort and some false starts before it starts to feel solid. There have been many times where I thought a group or friendship would lead somewhere but then petered out. Other times, a chance meeting has led to a deep friendship or a new hobby. So rather than counting on some specific things to work out, it's far better to keep an open, curious mind.

Your child's needs will naturally change over time. As they get older and have more independence, you'll no longer need to be quite so hands on, and you'll find a lot more freedom to go and explore yourself. A child may also go through different seasons. There could be times when a usually outgoing child feels like nesting for a while, and times where a more introverted child is particularly busy. One of the big advantages of community beyond school is that it is flexible and can shift as our children grow and change. I used to notice that there were moments where I felt like all our needs were being met, and then some kind of shift would happen (friendships change, people move away, groups end) and I'd feel the need to invest some energy again. This is just the natural ebb and flow.

> " In terms of community, I was really lucky at the beginning. I researched the local home ed community and met other mothers who were really welcoming, and that was amazing, but it could also be a challenge having four people who didn't all want to go to the same home ed group or who didn't all get on with other siblings." **HAYLEY**

> " We now have a couple of regular clubs we go to each week and ad hoc play dates with friends and that feels like enough for us right now. I think it's important for the boys to see other children in a home ed environment so they know they're not the only ones outside of school. They enjoy meeting new children, and for me it's really nice to meet other parents who are on the same path. I often find meeting just one parent can open up a whole new area of opportunities and experiences." **ANNIE**

Community for our children

How should community look for our children? The idea that school is essential for children to make friends and learn how to get on with each other is as ingrained in our collective consciousness as the idea that if you don't teach a child, they won't learn. You may well have family members or friends who are concerned about your child not getting enough social time with others, and this could be one of your own biggest fears. In this case, you may experience some guilt if you haven't managed to replace school with something that feels just as big and important for your children.

There is no doubt that building community is easier if your child enjoys going to different activities, likes to meet new people, and is of an age that they can be out and about by themselves. Compare that to having a younger child who may be recovering from an anxious time at school and who needs your presence to feel safe. Working out what feels right for your child is the best starting point. They might like to be with a couple of good friends, or they might like to do organized activities with lots of other children. I have friends whose children live for the next play date and friends whose children prefer a limited amount of social interaction with close friends.

> Everyone always says, 'What about socialization? What about friendships?' I let go of that by watching the relationships forming between my children and their friends, seeing how rich and meaningful they were. School friendships are different because they see each other every day, but my kids were playing together for hours, engaging in complicated, beautiful games. They might only see their friends once a week, but those interactions were meaningful." JAYNE

> My 11-year-old is in a football club and has lots of friends there who go to school, and she's friends with lots of home ed kids as well." HAYLEY

> We're all introverts, but Charlie is quite outgoing and needs a lot of human interaction. Once he's made the connection, that's that. Max is different and is less outgoing. I do worry about friendships and the social side, but I'm also astounded by their ability to know if a place or group is right for them." EVA

> It has massively opened my eyes. There's so much generosity of spirit in the ND [neurodivergent] community, and a wealth of thoughtful work and sharing of ideas, information and research. I've found so much support and I've ended up thinking that I'm glad this happened. I think there are a lot of preconceptions about home ed families. I met with a small group although my daughter wasn't ready to join in straight away, and I was struck by how accepting it was of children who need their own space. Every new person I meet has helped me. I feel like they put me back together again. My main recommendation is to try to find someone you can meet in person." RHONDA

The importance of autonomy

In Chapter 2 we talked about the huge value of autonomy, not just in learning, but in every aspect of our children's lives. Perhaps nowhere is that more important than in them having a voice in environments they move in and the people they engage with. Allowing them to go at their own pace, to feel into what feels safe for them and what feels overwhelming gives them the confidence to grow and to become discerning about themselves and what's right for them. Again, this may make our lives slightly more complicated, but this is valuable knowledge for them to acquire early on in life.

> I see in my daughter's friendship group that when that constant competition isn't there, they're free to just enjoy each other's talents without feeling like they should be able to do that too, or that they're not good enough. I think that sense of belonging and autonomy is important to cooperating." LIANNE

What community for ourselves looks like

It's normal for parents to find it hard going when their children have less need for community than they do. If you find yourself devastated that your child doesn't want to go to a weekly park meetup, chances are that there is more going on for you. It can take a while to find a balance that works for you all, and in the meantime, life can start feeling restrictive and lonely if your needs aren't being met. If that's the case, then finding ways to keep yourself connected is important. It can be challenging to balance our needs with our children's, but I do believe that being true to ourselves is the only way to go. For now, this may mean tending to your need for community without requiring your child to join in. Inviting a friend over to your home, connecting with online communities, or carving time out for your own activities while your partner or someone else is with your child – show your children how you're meeting your needs for connection so that when they're ready they can feel empowered to do the same.

On the flipside, if you have an extrovert child who loves to be with other people, but you yourself prefer solitude, you may find that you frequently need to push out beyond your comfort zone. It can be quite exhausting to be constantly meeting new people, so make sure to build in some downtime for you to recharge your batteries.

Meeting everyone's needs

Perhaps the most complicated piece in all this is meeting the needs of different people. Let go of how anyone else thinks things should look and think instead about how you each thrive as individuals. Creating something right for all of you isn't necessarily simple, but it's a wonderful opportunity to acknowledge your different needs and to work together. Accept that there will be much trial and error, and that that is absolutely fine. If you have more than one child you might have times when one is quite content but another feels like they need more action. Or if your children are young, you may need to figure out how to keep one sibling happy while the other takes part in a group or activity.

> Community can be tricky as it changes all the time. I've worried about it at points, and I can see how a lot of people miss the community at school and the friends. I've had to figure out what I need compared to what my children need. Sometimes I would want to go to a group just for my own socializing." CLAIRE

> Sometimes it can be a logistical nightmare. One really wants to get out and see a friend, and the other needs time at home, so it's a question of figuring out how this can all work. Then I call on community. One of my best friends lives next door and she unschools, so, I might be, like, can we stay with you while this one goes out, or can you pop over here while I do this? I don't have family nearby, and it would be really hard on my own. If you're a single parent you need your people, 100 per cent." HOLLY

> We found it relatively easy to find community through local Facebook groups, and this was really important to all three of us. It translated to long days of freedom and independence for my son and daughter, and lots of adult conversation for me. We all felt held by other families who were not in school, but were each 'doing' home education differently. There was never any sense of competition (which my two hated at school)." NICOLA

Don't compare yourselves to anyone else

As you do start to build your community, beware of thinking you need to be doing what everyone else is doing. It's great to see what others are up to and to get inspired, but don't let it become something to judge yourself by.

> " Talking to friends in the home ed community about how they were doing things helped. Initially, there was this feeling of 'we should be doing this or that'. But then I'd take a step back and think about it, and realize that some things weren't for us and that I didn't need to buy into the anxiety that some other people had. Acknowledging the big responsibility and gently looking after myself around that was part of the process." JAYNE

> " When the boys came out of school I went headlong into finding community and it slightly backfired! I went in too hard and tried to fill our days with home ed meetups when what they needed was time away from other children and space to adapt to a new way of life. I would also just flag that once you start hopping on home ed Facebook pages and WhatsApp groups, it's useful to remember that every family's learning journey is different. For example, if I saw a post asking for recommendations for a maths tutor for an eight-year-old, I'd instantly feel like that's what we should be doing and panic. At this point, I'd remind myself that this isn't relevant to our children's interests, and that's okay." ANNIE

Some tips for building your community

- *Keep an open mind.* Head along to events and activities that are going on locally, even if you're not sure it will be a good fit. You never know who or what's out there if you don't give it a go.

- *If something feels like a wonderful opportunity for your family, but your children are reluctant, it can be a good idea to go along by yourself, if possible, and get to know the people.* As we make and tend new connections, we are also building bridges for our children when they feel ready. Over the years, I've been to several groups and events without my children; eventually one of them might come along too, since it sounded like an enjoyable and friendly place to be. Or something else would come from the connection that did appeal to one of my children.

- *See if you can create something yourself.* It could just be an open invitation on a local home ed board to meet in a park, or perhaps you or your child has a special interest and you'd like to create a group around it. If you feel a bit reluctant to take the leap by yourself, maybe wait 'til you've met a couple of like-minded people, and then see if you can do something together.

> When we chose not to continue with school, I put an email out and 25 families turned up to the meeting. There's now a core group of five girls who became good friends. The girls are all very different – two have now gone to sixth form college, and one went back to school for the last years of secondary, but they all still get together." LIANNE

> I decided that instead of being fearful about some of their interests not being 'educational' enough, I would lean into them instead. I set up a Minecraft club in a cafe for young people to meet and play together. What has come out of it has been so valuable – new friendships, collaborating on amazing builds, supporting each other and sharing their knowledge. It's also been great for me to get to know other home ed families locally." ANNIE

- *Invest time in getting to know the people around you, and don't assume that the people you need in your lives must look just like you – the more varied your community, the richer the experience.* A huge benefit of community beyond school is that children get to hang out with adults and children of all ages. Children often feel more comfortable in mixed-age groups rather than peer groups. One of my children, who has attended a lot of home ed workshops and groups, was telling me the other day that they think that mixed-age groups often bring out the best in people.

- *While you are still building your in-person community, having some like-minded souls to talk with online can be extremely comforting.* This could be through a Facebook group or through an online community for parents who are exploring their own deschooling. A place to share worries and gain new perspectives can be a real lifesaver, particularly in the beginning, when there are likely to be a lot of doubts.

- *Don't compare with school!* Success isn't finding 30 peers for your child to hang out with all day. Success is continually looking to create something that feels good and healthy for you all.

The benefits of mixed-age groups

Research shows that there are many benefits for children of learning and socializing in mixed-age groups (Gray and Feldman 2004):

- *Social skills*. Mixed-age play encourages children to develop skills such as sharing, cooperation and negotiation.

- *Empathy and understanding*. Interacting with children of different ages helps children have a better understanding of diverse perspectives, needs and abilities.

- *Leadership and responsibility*. Older children often take on leadership roles, helping and guiding younger ones.

- *Reduced competition*. Mixed-age play tends to be less competitive, promoting cooperation and support over rivalry.

- *Learning opportunities.* Younger children learn new skills and concepts from older peers, while older children reinforce their knowledge by teaching.

- *Problem solving.* Children in mixed-age groups often engage in more complex play that requires advanced problem solving and critical thinking skills.

- *Emotional support.* Older children often give comfort and reassurance to younger ones, creating a nurturing and emotionally supportive environment.

- *Sense of belonging.* In the absence of competition, mixed-age play can foster a deeper sense of belonging. Everyone has a role and contributes to the collective fun and learning.

Journal prompts

- How would you imagine community could look for you and your child? How different are your needs?

- What community do you already have in place?

- How can you go about cultivating what you still need? What connections and opportunities are there near you?

Chapter summary

- Shifting to life without school can involve significant adjustments for families. It takes time for things to find their place, and both parents and children need support structures in place.

- Community is vital for emotional well-being and social connection, and many parents understandably feel a sense of loss on leaving a school community.

- Building a new community can take time and effort, but it gives parents the opportunity of building something intentional and wholly suited to their family.

- Some children may need more social interaction while others are content with less. It's important to respect and support our children's autonomy, so they can go at the pace they need.

- Parents should try to meet their own needs for community. If bigger groups are too difficult, aim for smaller things, and consider an online community to help support you.

References

Preface

Thomas, A. and Pattison, H. (2008) *How Children Learn at Home*. Continuum.

Introduction

Holt, J. ([1967] 2017) *How Children Learn*. Da Capo Lifelong Books.

Chapter 1

Cameron, J. and Pierce, W.D. (1994) 'Reinforcement, reward, and intrinsic motivation: A meta-analysis.' *Review of Educational Research* 64, 3, 363–423. www.jstor.org/stable/1170677?utm_source=chatgpt.com

Chaudhary, N. and Swanepoel, A. (2023) 'What can we learn from hunter-gatherers about children's mental health? An evolutionary perspective.' *The Journal of Child Psychology and Psychiatry* 64, 10, 1522–1525. doi: 10.1111/jcpp.13773.

Deci, E.L., Koestner, R. and Ryan, R.M. (2001) 'Extrinsic rewards and intrinsic motivation in education: Reconsidered once again.' *Review of Educational Research* 71, 1, 1–27. www.selfdeterminationtheory.org/SDT/documents/2001_DeciKoestnerRyan.pdf?utm_source=chatgpt.com

Di Domenico, S.I. and Ryan, R.M. (2017) 'The emerging neuroscience of intrinsic motivation: A new frontier in self-determination research.' *Frontiers in Human Neuroscience* 11, 145. doi: 10.3389/fnhum.2017.00145.

Gray, P. (2014) 'A survey of grown unschoolers 1: Overview of findings.' *Psychology Today*, Blog, 7 June. www.psychologytoday.com/us/blog/freedom-to-learn/201406/a-survey-of-grown-unschoolers-i-overview-of-findings

Gray, P. and Riley, G. (2014) *Grown Unschoolers' Evaluations of Their Unschooling Experiences: Report I on a Survey of 75 Unschooled Adults*. Boston College and Hunter College, US.

Immordino-Yang, M.H. (2015) *Emotions, Learning, and the Brain: Exploring the Educational Implications of Affective Neuroscience*. W.W. Norton.

Lahey, J. (2016) 'To help students learn, engage the emotions.' *The New York Times*, 4 May. https://archive.nytimes.com/well.blogs.nytimes.com/2016/05/04/to-help-students-learn-engage-the-emotions/index.html

Chapter 2

Ryan, R.M. and Deci, E.L. (2000) 'Self-determination theory and the facilitation of intrinsic motivation, social development, and well-being.' *American Psychologist* 55, 1, 68–78. doi: 10.1037110003-066X.55.1.68.

Rosenberg, M.B. (2015) *Nonviolent Communication: A Language of Life: Life-Changing Tools for Healthy Relationships*. Puddledancer Press.

Chapter 4

Holt, J. (2017) *How Children Learn*. Da Capo Lifelong Books.

Chapter 13

Cameron, J. (1995) *The Artist's Way: A Course in Discovering and Recovering Your Creative Self*. Pan Books.

Csikszentmihalyi, M. (1975) *Beyond Boredom and Anxiety: Experiencing Flow in Work and Play*. Jossey-Bass.

Csikszentmihalyi, M. (1998) *Finding Flow: The Psychology of Engagement with Everyday Life*. Basic Books.

Khoshnoud, S., Alvarez Igarzábal, F. and Wittmann, M. (2020) 'Peripheral-physiological and neural correlates of the flow experience while playing video games: A comprehensive review.' *PeerJ* 8, e10520. https://doi.org/10.7717/peerj.10520

Chapter 14

Gray, P. and Feldman, J. (2004) 'Playing in the zone of proximal development: Qualities of self-directed age mixing between adolescents and young children at a democratic school.' *American Journal of Education* 110, 2, 108–146. doi: 10.1086/380572.

Bibliography and Recommended Reading

Fisher, N. (2019) *Changing Our Minds: How Children Can Take Control of Their Own Learning*. Robinson.
Fisher, N. (2023) *A Different Way to Learn: Neurodiversity and Self-Directed Education*. Jessica Kingsley Publishers.
Gatto, J.T. ([1992] 2002) *Dumbing Us Down: The Hidden Curriculum of Compulsory Schooling (2nd edn)*. New Society Publishers.
Gray, P. (2013) *Free to Learn: Why Unleashing the Instinct to Play Will Make Our Children Happier, More Self-Reliant, and Better Students for Life*. Basic Books.
Griffith, M. (1998) *The Unschooling Handbook: How to Use the Whole World as Your Child's Classroom*. Three Rivers Press.
Holt, J. (1983) *How Children Learn* (Revised edn). Delacorte Press/Seymour Lawrence.
Holt, J. (1989) *Learning All the Time: How Small Children Begin to Read, Write, Count and Investigate the World, Without Being Taught*. Da Capo Lifelong Books.
Laricchia, P. (2012) *Free to Learn: Five Ideas for a Joyful Unschooling Life*. Living Joyfully Enterprises.
Laricchia, P. (2018) *The Unschooling Journey: A Field Guide*. Forever Curious Press.
Llewellyn, G. (2021) *The Teenage Liberation Handbook: How to Quit School and Get a Real Life and Education* (3rd edn). Lowry House Publishers.
McDonald, K. (2019). *Unschooled: Raising Curious, Well-Educated Children Outside the Conventional Classroom*. Chicago Review Press.
Natural Born Learners: Unschooling and Autonomy in Education. (2014). *Edited by Beatrice Ekwa Ekoko and Dr. Carlo Ricci*. CreateSpace Independent Publishing Platform.
Thomas, A. and Pattison, H. (2008) *How Children Learn at Home*. Continuum.

Unschooling memoires

Chen, I. (2020) *Untigering: Peaceful Parenting for the Deconstructing Tiger Parent*. [Self-published.]
Eldridge, L. and Eldridge-Rogers, A. (2017) *Jump, Fall, Fly: From Schooling to Homeschooling, to Unschooling*. FRC Press.
Obiols Llistar, M. (2021) *18: An Unschooling Experience*. Argyle Fox Publishing.
Richards, A.S. (2020) *Raising Free People: Unschooling as Liberation and Healing Work*. PM Press.